Human Rights and Fundamental Freedoms in Your Community

ASSOCIATION PRESS | NEW YORK

Stanley I. Stuber

Human Rights and Fundamental Freedoms in Your Community

Co-sponsored by the United Nations Association of the United States of America

DEDICATED TO | *Secretary-General U Thant*

Human Rights and Fundamental Freedoms in Your Community

Association Press, 291 Broadway, New York, N.Y. 10007

Co-sponsored by the United Nations Association
of the United States of America

Publisher's stock numbers: cloth, 1650; paper, 1653P
Library of Congress catalog card number: 68–11490

Printed in the United States of America

INTRODUCTION

A Basis for World Peace

The UN Universal Declaration of Human Rights is the inspiration and theme of this book, which is co-sponsored by the United Nations Association of the United States of America. Each chapter deals with one of the basic principles of this important document. And at the end of each chapter are two essential sections, one being questions for discussion purposes, and the other suggestions for action. While the book is intended for individual reading, its main purpose is to secure through group action solid implementation of the principles of the Universal Declaration.

By far the larger part of the source material used for the writing of this book has come directly from various agencies of the United Nations—documents, official reports, background papers, speeches and news releases. In addition, nongovernmental and voluntary agencies have supplied material. From this vast wealth of information I have attempted to update, summarize, and put in digest form material of special interest to the "ordinary" layman. I have also kept young people in mind in the preparation of the book, since it is expected to be used extensively in schools.

Another important source of material is the long and rich experience I have enjoyed in connection with the United Nations, beginning with its founding in San Francisco in 1945, where I served as an official representative for a world organization. Since then I have attended scores of UN meetings, including sessions of the Commission on Human Rights (especially at Lake Success when Eleanor Roosevelt was chairman), of UNESCO (in Mexico City and Paris), of the General Assembly (in Paris and at United Nations, New York), and of many specialized agencies (in Geneva and at United Nations, New York). I have also served as president of the Ridgewood, New Jersey, United Nations Association of the U.S.A., and was for several years a member of the UN speakers bureau in Kansas City, Missouri.

As a result of this close association with the United Nations through the years, I have come to appreciate the UN as a peacemaking organization. I have also come to realize that in this kind of world a large amount of positive understanding and creative cooperation among persons as well as nations is needed as a foundation for peacemaking. Therefore, this book is devoted to the "other side" of the UN—the work of technical assistance and the cultivation of human rights and fundamental freedoms. This essential operation, which is yet little recognized by the general public, seems to me to be of the utmost importance, especially in the crucial years just ahead.

While the book has no special "slant" and promotes no particular organization outside of the UN itself and its Universal Declaration of Human Rights, it does place emphasis upon the value of non-governmental and voluntary organizations for the implementation of human rights and fundamental freedoms. Now is the time for these organizations to take hold of causes represented in the Universal Declaration of Human Rights and support them in a big way. At this point the matter of UN information and the molding of public opinion in favor of the United Nations and its specialized agencies is of the utmost importance—not only to the United Nations but to the whole cause of world peace.

What Secretary-General U Thant said to the meeting of the World Council of YMCAs in Japan in 1965 also applies to many other voluntary agencies:

> The critical issues confronting the world today are the concern of all of us who have accepted the primary purposes enunciated in the charter of the United Nations—the maintenance of international peace and security and the well-being of mankind. As a voluntary agency, you are in a particularly advantageous and strong position to assist in a wider and better understanding of the United Nations. As increasing numbers of people across the world recognize the United Nations as the place where the hope of the human race is centered, the importance of effective dissemination of information cannot be exaggerated. Public opinion can be formed only by the dissemination of correct information, especially when it is undertaken by an organization such as yours with its influence in so many countries. The successes as well as the weaknesses of the United Nations must be interpreted in different ways in different areas of the world. It is of fundamental importance to the

work of the United Nations that the World Alliance of YMCAs, along with all non-governmental organizations which can help toward the creation of sound public opinion and public confidence, should exert itself in getting the facts before the peoples of the world. Aside from all other factors, support by an informed public is essential for the future success of the United Nations.

Directed toward these non-governmental and voluntary organizations all over the world, this book will, I hope, help them accomplish, to some larger degree, what Secretary-General U Thant considers so important.

STANLEY I. STUBER

CONTENTS

1. The UN Universal Declaration of Human Rights and Its Implementation

All human beings are born free and equal in dignity and rights. They are endowed with reason and conscience and should act towards one another in a spirit of brotherhood.

—From the UN Universal Declaration of Human Rights

The Universal Declaration of Human Rights

Adlai Stevenson said of Eleanor Roosevelt, the first chairman of the UN Commission on Human Rights, "She would rather light a candle than curse the darkness, and her glow has warmed the world." Because Mrs. Roosevelt represented in her life and work the human rights side of the United Nations, it is significant to note that in the UN gardens are two peace statues (in addition to the monument donated in her memory). One figure is a woman on horseback—symbol of peace—a gift of Yugoslavia. In her left hand she holds an olive branch; in her right hand, a symbol of the world. The other statue, a gift of the U.S.S.R., is a heroic, muscled male figure beating a sword into a plowshare.

The verse cut into the wall at the UN Plaza helps to give these statues extra meaning in a world of conflict and crisis:

> They shall beat their swords into plowshares, and their spears into pruning hooks; nation shall not lift up sword against nation, neither shall they learn war any more.

The UN Universal Declaration of Human Rights grew out of public demand for such a statement in much the same way as did the U.S. Bill of Rights. Representatives of many nations at the San Francisco Conference in 1945 spoke up to insist that the new organization include in its Charter an affirmative position on human rights. As a result the United Nations Chapter (adopted in October of that year) proclaimed "faith in human rights, in the dignity and worth of the human person, in the equal rights of men and women of nations large and small."

This, however, was only the first step. In order to define and to assist in achieving these principles, the Commission on Human Rights was established in 1946. Its first task was to draft a Universal Declaration of Human Rights. The assignment was completed nearly two years later, when the Declaration was adopted by the UN General Assembly (in 1948) by a unanimous vote (out of the fifty-eight nations then represented, forty-eight voted their approval, none voted against, two were absent). And in 1950 the General Assembly called upon "all states and interested organizations to adopt December 10 of each year as Human Rights Day." Over eighty nations now celebrate this day with special observances. In all this process the United States has been an active, moving force, keeping in mind that its own Declaration of Independence proclaimed the defense of "inalienable rights."

The Declaration consists of thirty articles, covering both civil and political rights and also economic, social and cultural rights.

Articles 1 and 2 are of a general nature, stating that "all human beings are born free and equal in dignity and rights" and are entitled "to all the rights and freedoms set forth in this Declaration without distinction of any kind such as race, sex, language, religion, political or other opinion, national or social origin, property, birth or other status."

The civil and political rights recognized in articles 3 to 21 include the following:

- the right to life, liberty, and security of person, including freedom from slavery and servitude and freedom from torture or cruel, inhuman, or degrading treatment or punishment;
- the right to recognition as a person before the law;
- the right to an effective judicial remedy; freedom from arbitrary arrest, detention, or exile;
- the right to a fair trial and public hearing by an independent and impartial tribunal;
- the right to be presumed innocent until proved guilty;

freedom from arbitrary interference with privacy, family, home, or correspondence; freedom of movement;
- the right of asylum;
- the right to a nationality;
- the right to marry and to found a family;
- the right to own property;
- freedom of thought, conscience, and religion; freedom of opinion and expression;
- the right of association and of assembly;
- the right to take part in government and the right of equal access to public service.

Articles 22 to 27 cover the following economic, social, and cultural rights:
- the right to social security;
- the right to work;
- the right to rest and leisure;
- the right to a standard of living adequate for health and well-being;
- the right to education;
- the right to participate in the cultural life of the community.

The concluding articles (28–30) recognize that everyone is entitled to a social and international order in which the rights and freedoms set forth in the Universal Declaration may be fully realized, and stress the duties and responsibilities which the individual owes to the community. The UN General Assembly proclaimed this Universal Declaration as "a common standard of achievement for all peoples and all nations" and called upon all its member nations and all peoples everywhere to promote and secure the effective recognition and observance of the rights and freedoms stated in the document.

Ever since its adoption the Declaration has exercised a profound influence throughout the world. The UN itself frequently quotes from it, or refers to it, in various resolutions representing standards to be applied. Several newly formed nations reflect its principles in their own constitutions. It has also influenced the national legislation and jurisprudence of a number of countries. The Declaration has inspired several international conventions or treaties concluded under the auspices of the United Nations. In the peace treaty concluded at San Francisco, Japan declared its intention to strive to realize the objectives of the Universal Declaration of Human Rights.

The entire human rights program that has developed, and is still developing in the United Nations has to a large extent been conceived within the framework of the Declaration. In fact, it can be fairly said that the purpose of the program of the whole UN organization is to promote the observance and implementation of the rights and freedoms set forth in this Universal Declaration of Human Rights.

The Formation of Covenants or International Treaties

It should be kept in mind that while the Universal Declaration of Human Rights represents a remarkable achievement in regard to the acceptance of common principles to be achieved, it has no legal status. In other words, it does not have the force of law; it is not a treaty. It derives its force as a statement of moral judgment, as a declaration of man's faith in himself, of belief in human dignity.

Having proclaimed this set of principles the UN centered its attention on a second step—the embodiment of these principles in the form of treaties that could be placed before member nations for their approval and ratification, and thereby become part of their national laws.

During the course of the years the UN (its affiliated agencies and bodies) has adopted several human rights conventions in order to implement the Universal Declaration of Human Rights, among which are these:

1. The Genocide Convention
2. The Convention on Slavery
3. The Convention on Forced Labor
4. The Convention on Women's Political Rights
5. The Convention on Equal Pay for Men and Women
6. The Convention on Discrimination in Employment
7. The Convention on Discrimination in Education

In addition to these conventions the UN General Assembly adopted on December 21, 1965, the International Convention on the Elimination of All Forms of Racial Discrimination. Adopted by unanimous vote, it represented two years of work. Secretary-General U Thant said at that time:

> Since the Universal Declaration of Human Rights was adopted and proclaimed on December 10, 1948, the world has anxiously awaited the completion of other parts of what was then envisaged as an International Bill of Human Rights, consisting of the Declaration, one or more international conventions, and measures of implementation. That is why the adoption of this Convention, with its measures of implementation set out in Part II, represents a most significant step towards the realization of one of the Organization's long-term goals.

The goal of which U Thant spoke was finally realized at the end of the UN General Assembly in December, 1966. For the first time in history, international protection for the basic rights of man was provided. This was done by the adoption of two covenants, or treaties, on human rights. These will, in due time, become legally binding on those countries that ratify them. They will come into force when thirty-five states have become parties. This represents a milestone in United Nations efforts to win universal recognition and respect for human rights. These covenants are as follows:

1. Covenant on Economic, Social, and Cultural Rights
2. Covenant on Civil and Political Rights
3. (Optional Protocol to the Covenant on Civil and Political Rights which concerns complaints from individuals)

For example, a country ratifying the Covenant on Civil and Political Rights would undertake to protect its people by law against cruel, inhuman or degrading treatment. It would recognize the right of every human being to life, liberty, security, and privacy of person. It would prohibit slavery, guarantee the right to a fair trial, and protect persons against arbitrary arrest or detention. The covenant also recognizes freedom of thought, conscience, and religion; freedom of opinion and expression; the right of peaceful assembly; and freedom of association. Other articles provide for freedom of consent to marriage and for protection of children. Preservation of the cultural, religious, and linguistic heritage of minorities is guaranteed.

A nation ratifying the Covenant on Economic, Social, and Cultural Rights would acknowledge its responsibility to promote better living conditions for its people. It would recognize everyone's right to work, to fair wages, to social security, to adequate standards of living and freedom from hunger, and to health and education. It would also undertake to protect the right of everyone to form and join trade unions.

Both of these covenants recognize the right of peoples to self-determination and have provisions barring all forms of discrimination in the enjoyment and exercise of human rights.

The unanimous vote creating this common bill of rights did not come easily. The first drafts of these covenants were submitted in 1955. (This was seven years after the General Assembly proclaimed the Universal Declaration of Human Rights.) It took another ten years to work out the final draft the nations could accept.

One other encouraging action in the progress of human rights took place at the twenty-third session of the Commission on Human Rights held in Geneva in 1967. It was the adoption of a convention on the elimination of all forms of religious intolerance, which will go to the General Assembly for final approval. This new measure seeks to safeguard freedom of conscience for both the believer and the nonbeliever, and their right to worship or to refrain from worship. It pledges nations which sign the convention to take positive steps against religious bigotry, including anti-Semitism.

Ambassador Patricia R. Harris, the U.S. Representative in Committee III of the United Nations, has declared,

> The International Covenants on Human Rights testify to our efforts to translate the principles set forth in the Universal Declaration into rights recognized in law. The importance of such efforts cannot be over-emphasized if we are to fulfill the hope voiced by Eleanor Roosevelt when she said that the Universal Declaration "might well become the International Magna Carta of all mankind . . ."

The Need for Ratification

It is one thing to get these conventions and covenants adopted by the United Nations itself; it is quite another thing to get them adopted by the governments that are members of the

UN. While a national delegation at the UN may vote for them, the government which has sent that delegation to the UN may not support it. For example, the United States delegation has signed, but the U.S. Senate has failed to agree to ratification.

This legislative gap is clearly pointed out in an editorial which appeared in the *St. Louis Post-Dispatch* of December 25, 1966:

> Obviously, there is a distance between voting for and signing United Nations treaties involving the rest of the globe and adopting them for the United States. The Executive branch agrees but the Senate does not commit. So the United States, in the end, praises but does not subscribe. The distance between the two may not be as far as from here to the moon, but it seems to be taking longer to cover it.

President Kennedy, in July, 1963, asked the advice and consent of the Senate to the three UN conventions dealing with (1) the abolition of all forms of slavery, (2) the abolition of forced labor, and (3) the political rights of women. His message to the Senate, in view of the current situation, deserves our special attention:

> United States law is, of course, already in conformity with these conventions, and ratification would not require any change in our domestic legislation. However, the fact that our Constitution already assures us of these rights does not entitle us to stand aloof from documents which project our own heritage on an international scale. The day-to-day unfolding of events makes it ever clearer that our own welfare is interrelated with the rights and freedoms assured the peoples of other nations.
>
> These conventions deal with human rights which may not yet be secure in other countries; they have provided models for the drafters of constitutions and laws in newly independent nations; and they have influenced the policies of governments preparing to accede to them. Thus, they involve current problems in many countries.
>
> They will stand as a sharp reminder of world opinion to all who may seek to violate the human rights they define.

They also serve as a continuous commitment to respect these rights. There is no society so advanced that it no longer needs periodic recommitment to human rights.

The United States cannot afford to renounce responsibility for support of the very fundamentals which distinguish our concept of government from all forms of tyranny. Accordingly, I desire, with the constitutional consent of the Senate, to ratify these conventions for the United States of America.

William Korey wrote in *Foreign Affairs* magazine for April, 1967, that

from 1945 to 1948 the United States delegation led the movement for the enactment of the Declaration (of Human Rights) as the embodiment of basic democratic political ideas. But since then, while the United Nations has been struggling to establish global norms of conduct, the United States has been the chief laggard in translating them into international law. At the present time the U.S. Senate has yet to ratify a single human rights treaty.

In speaking before the Ad Hoc Subcommittee of the Senate Foreign Relations Committee on Human Rights, March 8, 1967, Professor Richard N. Gardner of Columbia University was even more specific. He emphasized the fact that an inventory taken in the fall of 1966 revealed that only five of the 118 nations, members of the UN in 1948 when the Universal Declaration of Human Rights was adopted, had failed to ratify any of the UN conventions on human rights: the Maldive Islands, Spain, the Union of South Africa, Yemen —and the United States.

There are signs that the gap between the U.S. delegation at the UN and support the U.S. Senate gives is beginning to narrow. Ambassador Arthur J. Goldberg, speaking to the same Senate subcommittee in 1967, pointed out that "the Administration strongly supports ratification of these conventions." He then went on to say, "It believes them to be important agreements, to which the United States should adhere."

After reminding the subcommittee that the United States is already committed to the conventions in principle, Ambassador Goldberg declared,

I would point out, too, that ratification of these conventions would accord with our commitment to the Charter of the United Nations and to the principles for which it stands. . . . Countless times the United States has spoken publicly in support of the Charter and, specifically, in support of its human rights provisions. Why should we hesitate to ratify conventions that give such provisions a real meaning and force?

Apparently the answer to Ambassador Goldberg's question centers in U.S. public opinion. Not enough voters have registered their positive opinion in favor of U.S. ratification —at least not enough to impress enough senators. Many groups are now increasing their messages to the Senate favoring ratification. These include church, civic, labor and UN-related groups like the United Nations Association of the U.S.A. For example, the National Board of the Young Women's Christian Association of the U.S.A. sent this word to the Senate in March, 1967: "We hope most earnestly that the Senate will do its utmost to help restore some measure of our lost leadership and to absolve us from any charge of paying no more than lip service to human rights." The National Council of the Churches of Christ in the U.S.A. has declared,

> We believe that our nation can and must make its rightful contribution, along with others, by helping to develop international agreements such as the draft covenants on Human Rights and by ratifying others already in existence, such as the conventions for the political rights of women; for consent, age, and registration of marriage; against genocide, against slavery; and against forced labor.

The Women's Branch of the Union of Orthodox Jewish Congregations of America has urged its membership to "write to the United States Senators from your state, urging them to see that the Human Rights and Genocide Convention is brought to the floor of the U.S. Senate and to fight for its passage."

Morris B. Abram, U.S. delegate to the UN Commission on Human Rights, says that "one can only hope that the Senate will respond soon to the President's call for ratification of the genocide and the other pending conventions."

* * *

The remainder of this book, set against the background provided by this chapter, will be devoted to the implementation of the UN Universal Declaration of Human Rights. The focus for implementation will be increasingly sharpened, reaching down into every single local community.

The problem of implementation is a difficult one, and it is only fair to point out that the international treaties have failed to be implemented because of strong convictions by the opposition. And while the United States has not yet ratified the treaties, it has, nevertheless, been out in front in the practical day-by-day application of the principles propounded in the Universal Declaration. Therefore, while we work for treaty implementation we must also consider the arguments of the opposition and be fair to all concerned.

Questions for Discussion

1. What are the most important points stressed in the UN Universal Declaration of Human Rights?
2. Can these rights be reconciled with the Bill of Rights of the U.S. Constitution?
3. What are some of the ways in which the UN Universal Declaration of Human Rights can be implemented?
4. Why are "civil rights" and "human rights" often thought of as the one and same thing?
5. Should not the covenants (treaties) of the UN Universal Declaration of Human Rights, which have been placed officially before the U.S. Senate, be acted upon immediately?
6. Why have these covenants not been acted upon?
7. How can public opinion play a major part in getting these covenants adopted?

Suggestions for Action

1. Visit the United Nations headquarters.
2. Check with your church or synagogue to discover

whether it has done something to implement the UN Universal Declaration of Human Rights.

3. Join the United Nations Association of the U.S.A. (UNA–USA).

4. Write your U.S. Senator to register your opinion regarding the covenants and tell him of your desire to bring the covenants out of committee and to a vote.

5. Form a panel discussion group; hold a public meeting on the issues presented in this chapter; get organizations connected with UNA–USA to support the meeting.

6. Place a copy of the UN Universal Declaration of Human Rights in your school, church, or office; get it printed in your local newspaper during the International Year for Human Rights.

Note: The U.S. Senate ratified the Convention on Slavery on November 2, 1967, but not the other international conventions.

2. Intolerance, Discrimination, and Persecution

> Disregard and contempt for human rights have resulted in barbarous acts which have outraged the conscience of mankind, and the advent of a world in which human beings shall enjoy freedom of speech and belief and freedom from fear and want has been proclaimed as the highest aspiration of the common people.
>
> —From the UN Universal Declaration of Human Rights

In a study of the United Nations on "Discrimination in the Matter of Religious Rights and Practices" this sentence stands out:

> Although traditional forms of discrimination have now disappeared in most parts of the world because of the change in opinion of churches, of Governments, and of the general public towards dissenters—and above all because of the change in climate of the world community—a reversal of these happy trends (towards understanding and freedom) cannot be ruled out in the future.

We now appreciate how realistic this prediction is. In fact, just after the UN study was completed there occurred manifestations of anti-Semitism and other forms of racial prejudice and religious intolerance which cause concern to the international community. This is noted in a long footnote to the document (page 60).

The future, based on the past and present, does not appear too hopeful in regard to the elimination of intolerance, discrimination, and persecution. It is hoped that these manifestations of persecution of one kind or another do not represent part of a trend towards intolerance. In any event, as the UN document says, "the price of freedom of thought, conscience and religion, like that of all other freedoms, is eternal and increasing vigilance."

The International Convention on the Elimination of All Forms of Racial Discrimination

Secretary-General U Thant, in welcoming the formal approval of this convention, pointed out that it represents a significant step towards the achievement of goals proclaimed in the UN Charter because it not only calls for an end to racial discrimination in all its forms, but also goes on to take the steps necessary in establishing the international machinery to achieve this aim. He also indicated that it was a step toward the realization of an "International Bill of Human Rights."

This document, adopted unanimously by the UN General Assembly on December 21, 1965, after two years of work, though far too long to reproduce here, is summarized because of its historic importance.

After stating in a preface the reasons for having such a convention, it goes on to say, "Considering that the Charter of the United Nations is based on the principles of the dignity and equality inherent in all human beings" and "Considering that the Universal Declaration of Human Rights proclaims that all human beings are born free and equal in dignity and rights and that everyone is entitled to all the rights and freedoms set out therein, without distinctions of any kind, in particular as to race, color or national origin," and then proceeds to formulate specific articles.

Part II of the document spells out in several articles the formation and functions of a Committee on the Elimination of Racial Discrimination.

Part III, also with several articles, goes into detail regarding the method for signature of the document. As of September 15, 1967, sixteen nations had ratified this convention.

Various Forms of Discrimination

Discrimination takes many different forms; the most critical of these will be presented here at some length.

The UN Sub-Commission on Prevention of Discrimination and Protection of Minorities, at its nineteenth session, held at UN headquarters, January 4–23, 1967, adopted a resolution and a set of principles dealing with the following issues:

1. discrimination against persons born out of wedlock;
2. equality in the administration of justice;
3. racial discrimination;
4. violation of human rights;
5. freedom of information.

Discrimination Against Those Wishing to Leave or Enter a Country

A significant problem is that of the right of everyone to leave any country, including his own, and to return to his country without penalties. Discrimination against a person, or a group, leaving or entering a country is far more serious than most people realize (except, of course, those who get caught in the system). It is almost always of an indirect character and is administered by some form of government. Moreover, there is hardly a case where it is spelled out in national law or regulations. It occurs usually as a result of administrative action. Such action, far from being the result of the whim of a particular official, frequently is systematic and dictated by established governmental policy.

The most serious form of this type of discrimination occurs when citizens—with the exception of the ruler or members of a small governing clique—are not allowed to go abroad for any purpose whatsoever. This happens in time of revolution or war, declared or not. It often relates (in reverse) to news correspondents being refused admittance to restricted areas of the world.

Naturally, such discrimination is felt only by certain groups, and particularly by groups which differ in status from that of the predominant element of the population. Frequently denial of the right of everyone to leave a country has a spiraling psychological effect. Many individuals, for example, who are quite content to remain in a country as long as they know that they are free to leave whenever they choose, become anxious to get out as soon as they know that their freedom to do so is being denied. This is particularly true when they belong to a racial, religious, or other group being singled out for unfair treatment. Sometimes the physical effects of the denial of the right to leave a country are even more serious than the psychological ones. This is especially true in the case of a person seeking to leave a country because he is being persecuted. This, in fact, may be tantamount to the total deprivation of liberty, to imprisonment, or even to loss of life.

Anti-Semitism and Genocide

Anti-Semitism and the crime of genocide—the killing of a group of human beings—are closely related. Most people connect genocide, and rightly so, with the murder of millions of Jews in Europe under Hitler. But the problem is not confined to Hitlerism.

In a resolution unanimously adopted on December 11, 1946, the UN General Assembly affirmed that genocide is a crime under international law which the civilized world condemns. Then, on December 9, 1948, it adopted (again unanimously) a Convention on the Prevention and Punishment of the Crime of Genocide.

This convention defines genocide as the committing of certain acts with the intent to destroy, in whole or in part, a national, ethnic, racial or religious group per se. The actual acts constituting genocide are killing, causing serious bodily or mental harm, deliberately inflicting conditions of life calculated to bring about physical destruction in whole or in part, imposing measures intended to prevent birth, and forcibly transferring children. Also punishable under the convention are conspiracy or incitement to commit genocide, attempts to commit it, and complicity in the crime. The convention states that all who are guilty of genocide must be punished "whether they are constitutionally responsible rulers, public officers or private individuals."

Although the convention went into force on January 12, 1951, the government of the United States has not yet ratified it. Nations adhering to the convention are required to pass the laws necessary to give effect to it, and to grant extradition in cases of genocide. Those guilty of genocide are to be tried in the country where the crime was committed or by such international tribunals as may have jurisdiction. Any contracting party may call upon the organs of the United Nations to act under the UN Charter to prevent and suppress genocide as defined in the convention.

Racial Discrimination and Apartheid

"At this time, racial discrimination appears of greatest immediate danger to humanity," declared the World Conference on Church and Society (sponsored by the World Council of Churches) which met in Geneva in July of 1966. "It is often based not only upon fear or resentment of people of another color or tradition, but also upon economic self-interest."

Racial discrimination, though acute in the United States, is much more than a national problem; it is worldwide. Therefore the Church and Society Conference went on to say that

> the church and every Christian must redouble efforts to ease tensions between local citizens and strangers in their midst, at local and at national levels. It must encourage the legitimate aspirations of suppressed minorities and majorities, and support all practical measures aimed at changing any political and economic order which reflects the denial of political rights or economic opportunity, segregation, discrimination, or other oppression.

Racial discrimination has been condemned both by the World Council of Churches (in 1961) and by the Second Vatican Council (in 1965).

Dr. Joseph L. Lichten of the Anti-Defamation League of B'nai B'rith, writing in *The Catholic World* (March, 1966) maintains that

> the urgent need facing our communities, and the primary task in implementing the Declaration on Non-Christian Religions [of Vatican II], is education—an education which will eradicate distorted images from the thinking of both Christians and Jews, which will promote their confidence to approach and mingle with "the others," which will imbue both with the attitude that "We are Joseph, your brother."

Rabbi Arthur Gilbert has declared that

> a most heartening thing about the present situation is that Jews and Christians are beginning to meet one another in dialogue sessions, in shared study of biblical text, at the seminary level, and in the community. One can only anticipate that we shall soon see emerging a new understanding, a new theology of the nature of Jewish-Christian relationships.

"Civil rights," as applied in the United States, and "human rights," as used in connection with the principles of the UN Universal Declaration of Human Rights, while closely related, are nevertheless in different (although overlapping) spheres of influence. In the United States the term *civil rights* applies in the main to the Negro revolution which is now taking place and to which the Congress has passed legislation of a historic nature. In the context of the UN "human rights" include "civil rights," and the fundamental principles of the Universal Declaration of Human Rights ought to apply just as much to the United States as to any other nation. For this reason it is difficult to understand why a nation like the United States, which is struggling to give fair treatment to all its citizens regardless of color or national origin, should fail to ratify UN human rights conventions.

Few will admit that the Negro in the United States has achieved "equality" in any real sense. The substantial progress in race relations is still in the future. Yet, taking this into consideration, the whole case against discrimination (including discrimination against the Negro in the United States) will be advanced by accepting and by implementing the basic principles of the Universal Declaration of Human Rights and the international covenants and conventions on the elimination of all forms of racial discrimination.

The question of the policies of apartheid of the government of the Republic of South Africa has been before the UN, in one form or another, for many years. For example, from 1952 to 1960 the General Assembly made repeated appeals to the South African government to revise its policy on this question in the light of the principles of the UN Charter. In 1963 the Security Council called on all nations to stop the sale and shipment of arms, ammunition, and military vehicles to South Africa. In 1965 the General Assembly appealed to the major trading partners to stop their increasing economic collaboration with South Africa and renewed its call for a strict arms embargo. It also invited the specialized UN agencies to take measures aimed at compelling South Africa to give up its racial policies.

In 1965 the UN General Assembly also drew the attention of the Security Council "to the fact that the situation in South Africa constitutes a threat to international peace and security; that action was essential under Chapter VII of the UN Charter (which concerns measures the Security Council may employ when the peace is threatened or breached) and that universally applied economic sanctions were the only means of achieving a peaceful solution to the apartheid problem."

The Special UN Committee on the Policies of Apartheid of the Government of South Africa, at its 1967 meeting, decided to ask the UN Commission on Human Rights to take up the question of prison conditions in the Republic of South Africa and to give the widest publicity possible to the study prepared by UNESCO on the effects apartheid has on education, science, culture, and information in South Africa.

In 1967 the Commission on Human Rights, meeting in Geneva, adopted three resolutions in relation to racial discrimination: (1) It condemned the action of nations which by political, commercial, economic, and military cooperation encourage racist and colonial regimes in South Africa, in Portugal, and in Southern Rhodesia. (2) It decided to appoint a special rapporteur to make a survey of past United Nations action in its efforts to eliminate the policies and practices of apartheid in all its forms and manifestations; to study the relevant legislation and practices in South Africa, South-West Africa, and Southern Rhodesia; and to report back to the commission appropriate measures which might be taken by the UN General Assembly. (3) It decided that it would give annual consideration to the item "Question of violations of human rights and fundamental freedoms, including the policies of racial discrimination and segregation and of apartheid, in all countries, with particular reference to colonial and other dependent countries and territories."

Combat Racism in All Forms

At its 1967 meeting the Commission on Human Rights also concluded its consideration of a draft International Convention on the Elimination of All Forms of Religious Intolerance, and transmitted the texts of a preamble and twelve articles to the UN Economic and Social Council, which in turn referred the matter to the UN General Assembly. The General Assembly placed it on the agenda of its regular session in 1967.

On March 30, 1967, Chairman Achkar Marof, of Guinea, declared before the Special Committee on the Policies of Apartheid of the Government of South Africa that the purpose of the United Nations is to combat racism in all its forms wherever it occurs. He said that many resolutions have been adopted and many committees have dealt with the problem but nevertheless the situation throughout the world remains explosive and the menace of racism still acute. He pointed out that South Africa, a founding member of the UN, has persistently challenged the UN Charter and the spirit of the United Nations in matters relating to racial relations by adopting racist principles and promulgating oppressive and repressive laws. He emphasized the fact that the peoples of Africa are pledged to end racism on their continent. It is vital for the future of mankind, he maintained, that the so-called white nations join in the efforts of the other nations of Africa, Asia, and Latin America to combat racism in general and apartheid in particular.

*Freedom of Information**

A free mind, as related to freedom of the press and of information, has a direct bearing upon intolerance, discrimination, and persecution. For the withholding of such information or the deliberate slanting or editing of news can result in a cli-

* Freedom of information, although mentioned frequently in this book, especially in chapters 3 and 5, is not given a full treatment since it would require a book in itself. This issue is of the utmost importance, and the reader is urged to make a further study of its relationship to human rights. One good resource is the report of the UN Seminar on Freedom of Information held in New Delhi, February 20–March 5, 1962. Other material can be secured from UNESCO.

mate of false information, which leads to various forms of misunderstanding and persecution.

"Freedom of information is a fundamental human right and is the touchstone of all freedoms to which the United Nations is consecrated," the UN General Assembly declared in 1946. As a result, a conference on freedom of information was held in Geneva in the spring of 1948 to examine "the rights, obligations and practices which should be included in the concept of freedom of information." The UN drew up three conventions:

1. on the gathering and international transmission of news;
2. on the institution of an international right of correction;
3. on freedom of information. (This convention was on the agenda of the 1967 regular session of the UN General Assembly.)

Further work has been carried out by a special committee of five members appointed by the Commission on Human Rights in 1957 and by UNESCO (the purpose and work of UNESCO will be considered at length in Chapter 5).

Questions for Discussion

1. Why is there so much racial persecution in the world?
2. Who is to blame for this persecution?
3. How is racial discrimination ever to be overcome?
4. What did the Second Vatican Council do to create better race relations?
5. Why is religion in the Republic of South Africa such a serious continuing problem?
6. What is the UN doing to eliminate religious and racial persecution?
7. Who supports apartheid in South Africa?

Suggestions for Action

1. Go to a leader of another faith than your own and discuss with him how his group is trying to overcome religious and racial prejudice.
2. Discover what is being done about bias and prejudice in public school textbooks.

3. Call the Anti-Defamation League of B'nai B'rith and discover its present concerns.

4. Create a panel of speakers who will participate in public forums on a voluntary basis.

5. Circulate books and leaflets pointing out how prejudice can be overcome.

6. Form a panel discussion group; hold a public meeting on the issues presented in this chapter; get organizations connected with UNA–USA to support the meeting.

7. Check yourself against criteria contained in this chapter to discover how much racial prejudice you have.

3. Religious and Civil Liberty

> Everyone has the right to freedom of thought, conscience and religion; this right includes freedom to change his religion or belief, and freedom, either alone or in community with others and in public or private, to manifest his religion or belief in teaching, practice, worship and observance.
>
> Everyone has the right to freedom of opinion and expression; this right includes freedom to hold opinions without interference and to seek, receive and impart information and ideas through any media and regardless of frontiers.
>
> —From the UN Universal Declaration of Human Rights

Senator Charles H. Percy has declared (in *PTA Magazine*) that "political liberty is the most precious and most fragile heritage of Americans. Liberty is the theme of every one of our great founding documents, and liberty has been and continues to be what we live for and what we die for."

As the UN Universal Declaration of Human Rights emphasizes, "everyone has the right to freedom of thought, conscience and religion." In many ways the UN has been far in advance of religion itself in championing freedom in the modern world. Both the World Council of Churches and the Second Vatican Council, as we will discuss later in this chapter, have drawn upon the UN Universal Declaration of Human Rights for their support of liberty.

Besides serving as the greatest international forum, where vital issues of war and peace are discussed freely, the United Nations has laid down fundamental principles of liberty both by its action and by its various pronouncements on freedom. In its Universal Declaration of Human Rights it goes beyond the right to freedom of thought, conscience, and religion, to state that such a right also includes "freedom to change his religion or belief, and freedom, either alone or in community with others and in public or private, to manifest his religion or belief in teaching, practice, worship and observance." Moreover, it declares that everyone has the right to hold opinions and to express these opinions freely; everyone has the right to seek, receive and impart information and ideas through any media, regardless of frontiers.

UNESCO's Contribution to Freedom

United Nations Educational, Scientific, and Cultural Organization (UNESCO) by its constitution is to "contribute to peace and security by promoting collaboration among the nations through education, science and culture in order to further universal respect for justice, for the rule of law, and for the human rights and fundamental freedoms for all."

John S. Dickhoff, professor of higher education at the Center for the Study of Higher Education, University of Michigan, has said (in the PTA Highlight Series) that it is possible to restrict freedom of thought—although some maintain it cannot be done. He puts it this way:

> It is sometimes said that no one can restrict freedom of thought. We can think what we please. It was a seventeenth-century poet, Richard Lovelace, who said "Stone walls do not a prison make, nor iron bars a cage." But it is not quite true. Iron bars influence what one feels and thinks, and limit the experience about which one can think. Certainly they restrict movement. Restriction of speech is also restriction of thought. It is impossible to learn what we cannot read or hear. It is difficult to think what we cannot say or dare not say.

This is why the purpose and work of UNESCO are essential. The purpose of UNESCO is to contribute to the peace and security of the world by promoting active collaboration among the nations through education, science, and culture. This will be done in order to further universal respect for justice, for the rule of law, and for such human rights and fundamental freedoms as are affirmed for the peoples of the world without distinction of race, sex, language, or religion by the Charter of the United Nations.

Because UNESCO is so important to the mental, social, and cultural well-being of people everywhere the Prologue to the

UNESCO Constitution should be considered with special care. It reads in part as follows:

> The Governments of the States Parties to this Constitution on behalf of their peoples declare:
>
> That since wars begin in the minds of men, it is in the minds of men that the defenses of peace must be constructed;
>
> That ignorance of each other's ways and lives has been a common cause, throughout the history of mankind, of that suspicion and mistrust between the peoples of the world through which their differences have all too often broken into war.

The UN International Covenant on Civil and Political Rights

The UN International Covenant on Civil and Political Rights, adopted by the General Assembly on December 16, 1966, and implementing the fundamental principles of freedom expressed in the UN Charter and the Universal Declaration of Human Rights, presents international protection for the basic rights of man for the first time in history. As Secretary-General U Thant said when he officially welcomed the adoption of the covenants:

> On the occasion of the 1966 Human Rights Day, I had occasion to recall that in the philosophy of the United Nations, respect for human rights is one of the main foundations of freedom, justice and peace in the world. I pointed out that peace and respect for human rights go hand-in-hand. It is my sincere belief that our decision today will bring us nearer to the kind of a world which our Organization is committed to build. I earnestly hope that by early action, which Member States alone can take, the Covenants on Human Rights will soon become a living reality.

This International Covenant on Civil and Political Rights deals with the cause of religious and civil liberty in articles 18 through 27.

When this covenant is ratified, a part of its implementation will be the creation of a Human Rights Committee, consisting of eighteen members. The chief duties of this committee will be to receive reports and complaints from the various nations subscribing to the covenant, work with the UN Secretary-General in matters pertaining to human rights, and make reports to the UN Economic and Social Council.

The cause of human rights will be advanced to a large extent as this covenant is implemented. This is why citizens of the 122 member nations of the UN should press for its ratification. Although Roman Catholic, Protestant, and Orthodox religious bodies have now adopted similar principles, they do not possess the power of enforcement; unenforced principles are rather impotent. Religious bodies have now in this UN covenant a powerful support for their own publicly announced human rights principles dealing with freedom. They therefore have a new reason for working with and through the United Nations.

Religious Freedom and Human Rights

The American Council for Judaism declares that freedom is a natural right. "Only man eloquently strives for freedom," it says. "Pleas for freedom began as a small voice in man's ancient past; later, roared in Arabic and Hebrew as history's tyrants toppled. Tyrants reappear, but the voices of freedom each time rise to new crescendos." It continues, "First there is the grantor of freedom. Second is the grantee. Freedom—once granted—makes a demand of its own: the duty of the freed to act as freeman, seeing the larger society as his own, his own new birthright. Another dimension is the requirement of society to frame its laws and adopt its practices so that grantor and grantee are, forevermore, inextricably committed to raising all men higher by the bootstraps of freedom."

The World Council of Churches Commission of the Churches on International Affairs, in a 1965 statement, paid special tribute to the UN Universal Declaration of Human Rights in reaffirming the views on religious liberty as expressed by the World Council of Churches at Amsterdam in 1948 and New Delhi in 1961.

Along with this action by the World Council of Churches,

the official position adopted by the Second Vatican Council on December 7, 1965, takes on great historic significance, for this Vatican II action brings the entire Christian community of the whole world into unanimous support of the UN Universal Declaration of Human Rights.

In its Declaration on Religious Freedom the Second Vatican Council declared that

> the fact is that men of the present day want to be able freely to profess their religion in private and in public. Religious freedom has already been declared to be a civil right in most constitutions, and it is solemnly recognized in international documents. The further fact is that forms of government still exist under which, even though freedom of religious worship receives constitutional recognition, the powers of government are engaged in the effort to deter citizens from the profession of religion and to make life difficult and dangerous for religious Communities.

The late Father John Courtney Murray indicates that the document is a significant event in the history of the church. "Taken in conjunction with the Pastoral Constitution on the Church in the Modern World," he says, "the Declaration opens a new era in the relations between the People of God and the People Temporal. . . . Though the Declaration deals only with the minor issue of religious freedom in the technical, secular sense, it does affirm a principle of wider import . . . freedom. . . . The conciliar affirmation of the principle of freedom was narrowly limited . . . in the text. But the text itself was flung into a pool whose shores are wide as the universal Church. The ripples will run far."

Ripples have already reached as far as Spain. As a direct result of the Declaration on Religious Freedom of Vatican II, the Spanish government has adopted a new law regulating the exercise of civil rights in relation to religious liberty. It now grants (as of June 26, 1967) religious freedom, rather than mere toleration, to non-Catholics. Although Roman Catholicism is still the state religion, with special rights and prerogatives, and although the new law is still restrictive (disappointingly so), nevertheless in civil and individual rights Protestants and Jews (and those of no religion) take on the status of first-class citizens.

The U.S. Bill of Rights and the UN Universal Declaration

Those who live in the United States and enjoy a variety of freedoms under the Bill of Rights, amended to the U.S. Constitution, have a special reason to approve the principles of freedom as developed in the UN Universal Declaration of Human Rights. The UN Declaration extends to international relations the rights which the United States has enjoyed as a nation almost from its beginning.

For example, the First Amendment to the U.S. Constitution declares: "Congress shall make no law respecting an establishment of religion . . ." While there is a wide variation of interpretation regarding this part of the First Amendment, it is generally recognized that it guarantees a free church in a free state and that it gives every citizen the right to his own religion without interference by the government or by any group of citizens. And as James Madison put it: "The civil rights of none shall be abridged on account of religious belief or worship, nor shall any national religion be established, nor shall the full and equal rights of conscience be in any manner or on any pretext infringed."

The Most Precious of Human Rights

We should keep in mind two basic facts: (1) Freedom of thought, conscience, and religion represents the most precious of our human rights. (2) These rights have a direct bearing on all the other principles found in the UN Universal Declaration of Human Rights.

Arcot Krishnaswami, special rapporteur of the UN Sub-Commission on Prevention and Protection of Minorities, supports this conclusion in his report of a study he made of discrimination in the matter of religious rights and practices:

> The right to freedom of thought, conscience and religion is probably the most precious of all human rights, and the imperative need today is to make it a reality for every single individual regardless of the religion or belief that he professes, regardless of his status, and regardless of his condition of life.

Questions for Discussion

1. Why is religious freedom a key to other freedoms in the community?
2. How do the "Four Freedoms" (freedom from want; freedom from fear; freedom of speech and expression; freedom of worship) apply to the UN Universal Declaration of Human Rights?
3. What are the main points contained in the Declaration on Religious Freedom of Vatican II?
4. Why is there such a gap between freedom pronouncements and actual practice?
5. In what ways has Spain implemented the Declaration on Religious Freedom of Vatican II?
6. How free is the secular press?
7. What freedoms (other than religious and racial) are being violated today? Where? And how much?

Suggestions for Action

1. Go to your rabbi, pastor, or priest and ask him to explain to you, in brief, the history of persecution of his faith.
2. Read a book (perhaps from your public library) on the persecution of Jews.
3. Ask the editor of your local paper to explain why freedom of the press is so essential.
4. Monitor TV programs for a month to determine whether there is any apparent bias in any of the programming.
5. Form a panel discussion group; hold a public meeting on the issues presented in this chapter; get organizations connected with the UNA–USA to support the meeting.
6. List the basic principles of the U.S. Bill of Rights over against those in the UN Universal Declaration of Human Rights.

4. The Status of Women and Children

Men and women of full age, without any limitation due to race, nationality or religion, have the right to marry and to found a family. They are entitled to equal rights as to marriage, during marriage and at its dissolution.

Marriage shall be entered into only with the free and full consent of the intending spouses.

The family is the natural and fundamental group unit of society and is entitled to protection by society and the State.

Motherhood and childhood are entitled to special care and assistance. All children, whether born in or out of wedlock, shall enjoy the same social protection.

—From the UN Universal Declaration of Human Rights

The concerns of women, children, and the family are linked together in this chapter because they have a common basis for our serious consideration. It is true that for many years before the UN Universal Declaration of Human Rights was formulated there were champions of rights for women and children, particularly in political and economic areas. Nevertheless their concerns had never been put into international law until December 16, 1966, when they became a part of the International Covenants on Human Rights voted by the UN General Assembly.

The Culmination of Decades of Concern

One way to realize to what extent women and children have gained social, political, economic and legal status in the modern world is to check through, sentence by sentence, the two International Covenants on Human Rights adopted by the UN General Assembly on December 16, 1966. Here is the culmination of decades of concern for the equal rights of women. Here is a legal status for children which reflects the highest type of morality of the the twentieth century.

It is, of course, impossible to quote at any length all the references to women and children in these documents. Such terms as *everyone, all peoples, the right of everyone, any person, every human being,* and *no one* run throughout the documents, indicating that the rights and laws apply to everybody—men and women alike.

In regard to children the International Covenant on Economic, Social, and Cultural Rights says in part: "Special measures of protection and assistance should be taken on behalf of all children and young persons without any discrimination for reasons of parentage or other considerations. Children and young persons should be protected from economic and social exploitation."

Responsibility of Many Organizations

The responsibility for the rights of women and children rests with several bodies within the United Nations. For example, three of the six principal organs of the world organization include the question of the status of women, namely, the General Council, the Economic and Social Council, and the Secretariat—together with the Commission on the Status of Women, which is a subsidiary body of the Economic and Social Council. These work together to translate into action the fundamental principles of the UN Charter and the Universal Declaration of Human Rights.

The one organ of the UN in which all of the 123 member nations are represented is the General Assembly. It has powers and functions with respect to all other United Nations bodies. Among many other tasks, it has responsibility for carrying out the work of the UN for the promotion of universal respect for and observance of human rights and fundamental freedoms for all—without distinction as to race, sex, language, or religion.

The Economic and Social Council is directly responsible for the rights of women and children. Working under the authority of the General Assembly, it has responsibility for the promotion of human rights as one aspect of the UN program related to the development of international economic and social cooperation. Some of its specific functions are (1) making recommendations to promote respect for and observance of human rights and fundamental freedoms; (2) preparing draft treaties on matters within its competence and submitting them to the General Assembly; (3) coordinating the activities of the specialized agencies of the UN; and (4) arranging for consultation with non-governmental organizations concerned with matters related to the directions given to the Economic and Social Council. It also creates various commissions to help it carry out certain aspects of its work, the Commission on Human Rights and the Commission on the Status of Women being two of them.

The Commission on the Status of Women, which came into existence in 1946, is the functional body charged with improving the status of women in the political, civil, legal, economic, social, and educational fields. It also implements the principle that men and women shall have equal rights. It is therefore largely through the recommendations of this commission that both the General Assembly and the Economic and Social Council put into official action the implementation of human rights and fundamental freedoms—through the office of the UN Secretariat.

Recommendations of the Commission on the Status of Women

Through the years since 1946 the Commission on the Status of Women has initiated many recommendations which have finally been adopted by the United Nations in support of the Universal Declaration of Human Rights.*

Political rights are particularly important for women due to the fact that only through participation in the legislative, executive, and judicial organs of government can women obtain equality in other areas. The Commission on the Status of Women has taken several measures to promote equality in political rights. Of special importance is the Convention on the Political Rights of Women adopted by the UN General Assembly on December 20, 1952.† This was the first instrument of

* On November 7, 1967, the UN General Assembly adopted a Declaration on the Elimination of Discrimination against Women. The last of the articles (No. 11) reads as follows: "1. The principle of equality of rights of men and women demands implementation in all States in accordance with the principles of the Charter of the United Nations and of the Universal Declaration of Human Rights. 2. Governments, non-governmental organizations and individuals are urged, therefore, to do all in their power to promote the implementation of the principles contained in this declaration."

† This convention came into force on July 7, 1954. Thus far, fifty-three states (nations) have become parties to it.

international law aimed at granting and protecting women's rights on a worldwide basis. It provides (in those countries which are parties to the convention) that women shall have the right to vote, to be eligible for election, to hold public office, and to exercise all public functions on an equal basis with men.

Although the right of women to vote is now a reality in most countries, nevertheless throughout the world much remains to be done to secure full political equality, particularly in the wide field of access to public office.

The Commission on the Status of Women has also been concerned with the question of the education of women. In close cooperation with UNESCO and the International Labor Organization, it has initiated various studies on the access of girls and women to education at all levels; on the access of women to the teaching profession; and on vocational guidance, technical, and professional training of girls and women. It has also advocated free and compulsory education for all, special measures to eliminate illiteracy among women, and the development of programs of adult education.

The commission has concerned itself with economic opportunities for women, including such issues as the equal remuneration of men and women for work of equal value. It has provided studies on various aspects of the economic rights of women: part-time work; the employment of older women workers; opportunities for women in cottage industries and handicrafts; the position of working women (including women with family responsibilities); the age for retirement and the right to a pension.

In the area of tax legislation applicable to women, the Economic and Social Council has supported the position taken by the Commission on the Status of Women that legislation should provide for equal treatment of men and women in regard to taxation of earned income.

One area in which women do not enjoy equality with men is that of private law—especially family law and property rights. Many legal systems throughout the world do not permit mothers any voice in bringing up their own children, nor allow them guardianship upon the father's death. The wife's civil capacity has been restricted in many nations, and she is allowed no legal domicile other than her husband's. In some countries women lose property rights upon marriage, and do not have equal rights relating to inheritance. After extensive studies of such situations the Commission on the Status of Women has recommended that governments take all possible measures to provide for the equality of rights and duties of husband and wife in conformity with the Universal Declaration of Human Rights. Special recommendations such as the following were also adopted by the Economic and Social Council:

1. equal parental rights and duties;
2. a married woman's right to have a legal domicile other than her husband's;
3. the right of a married woman to work outside the home without her husband's authorization;
4. statutory matrimonial property systems giving women equal rights over separate and common property during marriage as well as an equitable share of property after the dissolution of marriage;
5. equality of inheritance rights of men and women.

The UN General Assembly in 1954 endorsed the position of the Commission on the Status of Women by recommending that all nations take the necessary measures for the abolition of such customs, laws, and practices as affect the dignity of women as human beings and are inconsistent with the UN Charter and the Universal Declaration of Human Rights. On the basis of studies and recommendations the commission made on marriage—with particular regard to free consent to marriage, minimum age for marriage, and registration of marriage—the UN General Assembly adopted on November 7, 1962, the Convention on Consent to Marriage, Minimum Age for Marriage, and Registration of Marriages.* It provides that no marriage shall be entered into without the full, free consent of both parties; that nation parties to the convention shall undertake to prescribe a minimum age for marriage; and that all marriages shall be registered by a duly constituted authority.

The Convention on the Nationality of Married Women, adopted by the UN General Assembly on January 29, 1957, provides, on the one hand, that marriage to an alien shall not automatically affect the nationality of the wife and, on the other, for special privileged naturalization procedures for a wife who wishes to take the nationality of her husband.†

* This convention came into force on December 9, 1964. Thus far, seventeen nations have ratified it.

† This convention came into force on August 11, 1958. Thus far, thirty-six states have ratified it.

At its 1967 session the Commission on the Status of Women also adopted resolutions on the political and economic rights of women, access to education, parental rights, discrimination against persons born out of wedlock, and periodic reports on human rights. It also called upon all those responsible "for the fate of peace to exert all their efforts to prevent aggression and armed intervention and to eliminate the hotbeds of war in the world."

Birth Control and Family Planning

In 1966 the Commission on the Status of Women prepared a statement which recognized the program of work recommended by the UN Population Commission and the interest of UNESCO in strengthening and broadening proposed programs in demography, and then went on to say:

> [This commission,] *believing* that expanded research with regard to family planning will be of great value, and that educational information which can be expected to result from this research should be available to women in developed as well as in developing countries,
>
> 1. *Invites* the Secretary-General to include in the report he is preparing for the twentieth session of this Commission on the relation between family planning and the advancement of women, a brief summary of pertinent research and resources available through the United Nations, with special emphasis on informational material which might be used in conferences of non-governmental as well as of official bodies;
>
> 2. *Welcomes* the increasing recognition of the role of United Nations agencies in providing assistance, upon the request of Governments, in educational programmes concerned with the planning of families.

The General Board of the National Council of Churches in 1963 made a statement in support and ratification of the UN position.

At the World Conference on Church and Society, sponsored by the World Council of Churches during July of 1966 in Geneva, a statement was adopted, which read in part:

> A woman's life, like a man's, is lived in stages. But child-bearing and child-rearing occupy much less of her time than

formerly, as she has fewer children and there is more schooling outside the home. Woman's role in contemporary society is to realize her individuality. There is no single role for women any more than there is for men. For some their proper place is in pursuit of a career which has traditionally been considered the male domain; for others it is still that of wife and homemaker. Women need and have a right to training for non-domestic work. They do not want to be treated as men, and men—if they are wise—will not expect women to conform to male patterns of work arrangement.

Women and Children Together

The welfare of women and children is closely connected. The UN Declaration of the Rights of the Child states: "The best interests of the child shall be the guiding principle of those responsible for his education and guidance; that responsibility lies in the first place with his parents."

The Work of UNICEF

One of the most popular aspects of the work in behalf of children within the United Nations is UNICEF (United Nations Children's Fund). Established on December 11, 1946, by the UN General Assembly to help developing nations improve the condition of their children and youth, UNICEF aids national projects, assisting countries only at the request of their governments.

The Fund offers help in such areas as health, nutrition, social welfare, education, and vocational training. It also helps governments to assess the major needs of their young people and plan comprehensive programs to meet them.

A large part of the UNICEF operation takes the form of providing equipment and supplies; health center equipment, drugs, well-digging rigs, dairy-plant equipment, school garden supplies, and equipment for the production of textbooks are typical. UNICEF also delivers surplus milk powder donated by several nations for use chiefly in health centers. And UNICEF provides assistance training programs at all levels—from the simplest form of practical training for auxiliary workers in disease-control campaigns to post-graduate studies.

The status of UNICEF within the United Nations is semi-autonomous; the largest source of its income is from voluntary government contributions. Nevertheless, considerable income comes from other sources, mainly from groups and individuals. The sale of UNICEF greeting cards totals millions of dollars annually.

It is significant to note that UNICEF was given the Nobel Peace Prize in 1965.*

In many developing countries the government cannot provide schools or teachers to half the children of school age. This can create a "lost generation" unless extra help is given, declared Henry R. Labouisse, director of UNICEF, on December 8, 1967.

The World's Children

The work of UNICEF is tied directly to the tragic needs of the children of the world, particularly those in underdeveloped areas. For example, a report of the Conference on Children and Youth in National Planning and Development, held in Bangkok in 1966, stated in part:

> At least one-half of the countries in Asia have incomes which fall below the levels necessary for maintaining minimal standards of consumption of the basic necessities of life. At least two-thirds of all Asian children live in families which are poorer and larger than average families. Millions of children suffer from parasites and infectious diseases. Around 60% in the age group of 15 and above are illiterate; and illiteracy is particularly acute in rural areas, especially among women.

The Declaration of the Rights of the Child

The United Nations first indicated a real interest in a declaration on the rights of children in 1946. Inspired by the Declaration of Geneva—which the Assembly of the League of Nations adopted in 1924—a recommendation was made to the UN Economic and Social Council that this Geneva Declaration "should bind the people of the world today as firmly as it did in 1924." Two of the commissions of the council—the Social Commission and the Commission on Human Rights—were made responsible for the preliminary drafting of a new UN

---

* Those who want the full story of UNICEF's remarkable service should see "Window on the Future," a booklet published by UNICEF.

declaration. The "Third Committee" of the UN General Assembly put the draft in its final form.

On November 20, 1959, the UN General Assembly adopted unanimously a Declaration of the Rights of the Child. Its preamble specifically states that the child, by reason of his physical and mental immaturity, needs special safeguards and care, before birth and afterwards. It also affirms that mankind owes to the child the best that it has to offer. Parents, individuals, voluntary organizations, local authorities, and governments are called upon to recognize the rights and freedoms set forth and to strive for their implementation. The declaration, further, affirms the following:

1. the right of all children to enjoy, without any exception whatever, special protection and to be given opportunities and facilities to enable them to develop in a normal and healthy manner and in conditions of freedom and dignity;
2. the right to have a name and nationality from birth;
3. the right to enjoy the benefits of social security, including adequate nutrition, housing, recreation, and medical services;
4. the right to receive special treatment, education, and care, if handicapped physically and mentally;
5. the right to grow up in an atmosphere of affection and security and, wherever possible, in the care and under the responsibility of their parents;
6. the right to receive an education;
7. the right to be protected against all forms of neglect, cruelty, and exploitation;
8. the right to be protected from practices which may foster racial, religious, or any other form of discrimination;
9. the right to be brought up in a spirit of understanding, tolerance, and friendship among peoples;
10. the right to be nurtured in the full consciousness that his energy and ability shall be devoted to the service of his fellowmen.*

---

* For a more complete study of women and children in relation to the United Nations, see the UN booklets "The United Nations and the Status of Women" and "Civic and Political Education of Women," along with the Declaration of the Rights of the Child. On August 2, 1967, the UN Economic and Social Council,

Questions for Discussion

1. What are the rights of children in the modern world?
2. How are children being kept from enjoying their natural rights?
3. Why are children much better off today than they were even a decade ago?
4. Where are children still being mistreated?
5. Why do we need to be concerned about the status of women?
6. What is the UN Commission on Human Rights doing to give women equal rights?
7. In what areas of life are women still at a disadvantage?
8. Describe some ways in which business and industry depends upon women today.

Suggestions for Action

1. Visit a "poverty area" to find out if the children are being cared for properly.
2. Get a local organization (such as the PTA) to have a panel discussion on "The UN and the Rights of Children."
3. Check with some business organizations to determine whether women receive equal pay for equal work.
4. Get your high school paper to run a model UN meeting on a human rights topic.
5. Form a panel discussion group; hold a public meeting on the issues presented in this chapter; get organizations connected with the UNA–USA to support the meeting.
6. Read the Declaration of the Rights of Children to some group in your community (or have it read from a pulpit or put on a bulletin board in a public place, such as a YMCA-YWCA or the public library).

---

meeting in Geneva, endorsed the policies and programs of UNICEF and urged governments and private groups to consider "as a matter of urgency" increasing their contributions to UNICEF so that its income goal of fifty million dollars would be raised by the end of 1969.

5. The Right to an Education

Everyone has the right to education. Education shall be free, at least in the elementary and fundamental stages. Elementary education shall be compulsory. Technical and professional education shall be made generally available and higher education shall be equally accessible to all on the basis of merit.

Education shall be directed to the full development of the human personality and to the strengthening of respect for human rights and fundamental freedoms. It shall promote understanding, tolerance and friendship among all nations, racial or religious groups, and shall further the activities of the United Nations for the maintenance of peace.

—From the UN Universal Declaration of Human Rights

"The demand for education is universal and irresistible," says René Maheu, Director-General of UNESCO.

"Since wars begin in the minds of men, it is in the minds of men that the defences of peace must be constructed," says the UNESCO Charter.

In these two sentences is summarized the purpose and accomplishments of the peace-making functions of UNESCO, which is one of the most essential operations of the UN. It has so many different aspects, undergirding the goal of universal education, that only a small part of it can be outlined here. Hopefully, the reader will be encouraged to learn much more about UNESCO and become one of its active supporters.

"Every child in the world must have a school to go to by 1970." Educational planning is proceeding under this motto. Yet planned education depends very largely upon the great basic freedoms—freedom to think, freedom of speech, freedom to read and freedom of conscience. Without these freedoms as an incentive and an objective it is doubtful whether the national planning of education would be carried along with much enthusiasm and support by the various governments. This is why the educational programs of UNESCO are so essential, since they operate not only in many practical ways to educate the people of the world, but also to create the cultural environment in which such training can be developed successfully. Two of UNESCO's goals are that "everyone has the right freely to participate in the cultural life of the community" and that all "education should be directed to the full development of the human personality." Therefore UNESCO has for its overall objective the promotion of "understanding, tolerance, and friendship among all nations, racial, or religious groups, and [the furtherance of] the activities of the United Nations for the maintenance of peace."

What Is UNESCO?

The three main tasks of UNESCO, according to its constitution:

1. to maintain, increase and diffuse knowledge;
2. give fresh impulse to popular education and to the spread of knowledge;
3. to collaborate in the work of advancing the mutual knowledge and understanding of peoples.

In order to understand the vast scope of UNESCO's varied activities it is essential to realize that its operations are carried out on several different levels at the same time. Although this is the case, three aspects stand out: international intellectual cooperation; operational action in service of developing areas; and moral action.

Beginning in 1946 with its basic charter of operation, UNESCO has developed its own program step by step from a distinction between its "general activities" and its "special activities," to many major projects. A priority was given in 1960 to education and in 1964 to science as factors in economic and social development.

In order to achieve its aims UNESCO collaborates in the work of advancing the mutual knowledge and understanding of peoples through all means of mass communication. It gives fresh impetus to popular education and to the spread of culture. It also encourages the teaching and understanding of science.

Specifically UNESCO's program includes the creating of favorable conditions for increasing international understanding by aiding man's access to education and culture, by uniting the efforts of scientists, artists, and educators, and by breaking down obstacles to the free flow of thought. Major programs include a literacy drive, teaching about the United Nations and human rights, compulsory education, and the raising of educational standards. They also contain exchange of persons and provision of scientific and educational experts on request of member nations.

Education: A Chief Factor in Development

In an address before the UN Economic and Social Council in 1965, René Maheu said:

> It is no longer necessary to prove that education is one of the basic factors, if not the basic factor in development. Man is both the instrument and the end product of development and his education is now a subject that has assumed increasing weight even in economic studies. If we compare 1965 with 1960 we find that this is perhaps the major innovation in thinking on development and in the strategy for development adopted by international organizations. I am convinced that this fact, now that it is universally acknowledged and affirmed, should be the major factor in shaping the future policy of these international organizations in the second half of the UN Development Decade.
>
> Without scientists, engineers and technicians at all levels no country can call itself free. This raises the whole problem of scientific and technical education, from secondary school study to basic research carried out at the higher institute level, taking in every type of technical training whether in or outside universities and schools within the framework of industry and agriculture.
>
> The idea of education no longer has to be promoted. The motivation for it exists already and springs from deep within the hearts of the great masses of humanity. This demand for education has not been created by international organizations or by governments. On the contrary, to many it must seem like some surging wave that threatens to sweep everything before it unless it is channelled in time into new paths where its vast potentialities can be rationally exploited. The need, the passion, for education is such that

it is turning into an irresistible clamour of world-wide dimensions sparked by the triple cry for national development, national freedom and respect for the dignity of man. So strong and far-reaching is this demand that many nations —be they highly developed or not, newly independent or established for centuries—now find themselves face to face with a host of formidable problems which are no longer just technical or even economic and financial in nature but also political.

The Universal Right to an Education

During the past two decades there has been an explosion in education. Significantly, during this same period, for the first time in history the claim has been made, and conceded, that every single human being on the face of the earth has a right to an education.

The right to an education was really enshrined in the Universal Declaration of Human Rights. Meeting in Beirut, Lebanon, in 1948, UNESCO's general conference hailed this "historic moment when the value of the human person was universally proclaimed" and "which would enable every man to develop his creative powers to the full benefit of all and in the cause of progress."

It is essential to realize that when the UN Charter was signed only a handful of people knew about the impending release of nuclear energy. This event opened up an entirely new era in human history. Because of it, our knowledge and control of nature have advanced more rapidly than the imagination can follow. Supersonic aircraft, space satellites, men in outer space, and even landings on the moon and other planets are almost taken for granted. Mass communications have revealed various developments of cosmic exploration.

The humanitarian sciences have also developed in a spectacular way. Moreover, there has been a renaissance in the area of environmental sciences such as meteorology, oceanography, and geology. Discoveries in physics have not only revolutionized warfare, but also brought unlimited energy for peaceful purposes. Transistors and computers have increased human mental efficiency a thousandfold.

In areas of ideas and events there has been progress. Many people have emerged into political freedom. International agencies have won more adherents. Understanding and co-operation have increased in certain areas. And while the general conclusion seems to be that because of scientific and economic advances mankind as a whole is making rapid progress, the final truth of the matter does not show a positive balance. The apparent progress is offset by new hatreds, bitter misunderstandings, and open warfare. The gap dividing the "have" and the "have-not" nations is growing wider. Nearly two thirds of the world's population still live near, or below, the subsistence level. The refugee problem, since the conflict in the Middle East, has increased to alarming proportions.

The obstacles present a challenge to education. We need many different kinds of education, especially via mass media, if the world situation is going to come out with a plus rather than a minus. And UNESCO, because of its many projects all around the world, offers one of the best avenues of hope. In the words of Miss Ellen Wilkinson, former British Minister of Education, who had much to do with the formation of UNESCO,

> Memorials will be raised—many of them—to the fighting men; but there are others for whom there will be no memorials and whose names, in many cases, are unknown. They died in the grim fight for the freedom of the human mind. . . . We who are carrying on their work and who are starting this right [through UNESCO] to carry on their work are doing it in the hope that we shall carry on the flame of their souls and spirits in the children and the young people who are committed to our care. Also at this solemn moment we say to the teachers of the world that those who fight in the struggle against ignorance and illiteracy do not fight alone; they fight with us behind them, with this great international organization [UNESCO] for them to appeal to.*

The Doctrine of Equality

As is pointed out in the UNESCO Constitution, "ignorance of each other's ways and lives has been a common cause,

---

* From her speech at the closing of the conference for the establishment of UNESCO (quoted in UNESCO *Newsletter*, February, 1947).

throughout the history of mankind, of that suspicion and mistrust between the peoples of the world through which their differences have all too often broken into war."

The constitution goes on to declare:

> The great and terrible war which has now ended was a war made possible by the denial of the democratic principles of the dignity, equality and mutual respect of men, and by the propagation, in their place, through ignorance and prejudice, of the doctrine of the inequality of men and races.
>
> The wide diffusion of culture, and the education of humanity for justice and liberty and peace are indispensable to the dignity of man and constitute a sacred duty which all the nations must fulfill in a spirit of mutual assistance and concern.
>
> A peace based exclusively upon the political and economic arrangements of governments would not be a peace which could secure the unanimous, lasting and sincere support of the peoples of the world, and peace must therefore be founded, if it is not to fail, upon the intellectual and moral solidarity of mankind.

Assistance for Development

The major part of UNESCO's work today is marked by the year 1950, for it was then that UNESCO was first able to send experts to the member nations of the UN, paid for under the United Nations Expanded Program of Technical Assistance.* The purpose of this project was to assist countries, at their own request, "to strengthen their national economy through the development of their industries and agriculture with a view to strengthening their economic and political independence in the spirit of the Charter of the United Nations and to ensure the attainment of higher levels of economic and social welfare for their entire populations."

As a result of this, UNESCO was able not only to advise UN member nations on what needed to be done but, if they so desired, to send experts to help them take action and also enable their nationals to benefit from the experience of others by studying in other countries.

* UNESCO, like other UN specialized agencies, cooperates with several United Nations organizations in carrying out projects.

Beginning in 1960 with the creation of the UN Special Fund, UNESCO, like the United Nations itself and other specialized agencies, was able to give decisive operational assistance to its member nations. The fund was established to encourage the flow of investment capital for economic expansion. It was recognized that as the full and rational mobilization of human resources was essential to economic expansion, so also projects for the development of education and science constituted basic investments for economic development.

When in 1965 the Special Fund and the United Nations Expanded Program of Technical Assistance were merged to become the UN Development Program, UNESCO became responsible for financial assistance to ninety-eight projects in fifty-eight nations. Most of these programs deal with higher technical and technological training, along with various literary projects.

By 1967 UNESCO had given assistance to over a hundred countries, totaling millions of dollars—chiefly in the fields of education and natural science. Work has been done more recently in certain areas of the social sciences, culture, and mass communication. A total of more than five thousand expert missions, for periods ranging from months to several years, have been provided under the Technical Assistance program. Hundreds of experts and fellowships have also been provided under UNESCO's regular budget.

Ethical Action

While UNESCO's program is utilitarian, its chief mission is ethical. Its major goal is to further respect for justice, for the rule of law, and for the dignity of man without distinction of race, sex, or religion. And this ethical purpose is reflected throughout all its technical action. The real justification for UNESCO's intellectual cooperation—beyond immediate usefulness—is the promotion of the awareness of mankind's intellectual and moral solidarity. Moreover, the rationale of operational assistance to economic development is the correction of injustices—through the relief of poverty and want.

The ethical purpose of UNESCO, which led its founders to affirm that "it is in the minds of men that the defenses of peace must be constructed," has been followed through special activities in education, social sciences, and culture. (The importance and effectiveness of these must not be measured in terms of the relatively small funds allotted to them.) Here it is recognized that the promotion of human rights, and the dignity of the individual, along with mutual appreciation of cultural values and of understanding between peoples so that tolerance, goodwill and a sense of justice govern their relations, are achieved by patient and increasing reflection, research, and education.

Also the International Convention and Recommendation Against Discrimination in Education, adopted in 1960 and translated into specific concepts, has led to action throughout the world, giving reality to ideals.

The preparation of universal standards which all nations can and should achieve, the scientific study of various relations between governments and peoples, the teaching of international understanding in schools, the diffusion and exchange of what is best in the cultures of all peoples, the campaign to bring new reading methods and materials to the illiterate—these are some of the ways in which UNESCO is helping to act on men's minds so as to turn them in the direction of international cooperation and toward the active pursuit of peace.

Mass Communications

In a brief chapter such as this it is impossible to do justice to the very extensive mass communication programs of UNESCO. The most that can be done is to summarize some of them and to encourage the reader to seek further information through UNESCO itself.

Recognizing that information is not only a "right," as the UN Universal Declaration of Human Rights declares, but also a basic necessity for both the individual and society, UNESCO is fully aware of the fact that mass media are absolutely essential to educational, scientific, and cultural development.

While the modern inventions in communications have been enormous—take the transistors in relation to radio and the space satellites in relation to television as examples—and while few people are now beyond the reach of the mass media of communication, yet their full potential has not been realized. As a recent UNESCO survey shows, a large part of the world's population, for diverse reasons, is still inadequately equipped with the means of information. In the developing nations, for instance, telecommunicational services are inadequate and expensive, capital for the establishment and expansion of information enterprises is lacking, and foreign currency with which to import newsprint, broadcasting equipment, raw film, and other materials is in short supply. The worst obstacle of all is a dearth of trained personnel.

All this is a challenge to UNESCO. And UNESCO is meeting the challenge, not only by providing the ways and means, but also by promoting the exchange of persons as an essential element both in the training programs and in the sharing of different geographical and cultural backgrounds—so necessary in reducing the lack of knowledge and understanding which so often leads to hostility.

UNESCO and the Book Revolution

Because of its mandate, UNESCO is naturally involved in the promotion of books and various kinds of printed materials. It is required by its constitution to promote "the free flow of ideas by word and image" and also to "give the people of all countries access to the printed and published materials produced by any of them." The 1964 general conference of UNESCO therefore placed particular emphasis upon publications for the promotion of mutual understanding, and economic and social development. It also recognized the need to strengthen international cooperation in regard to the publishing and distribution of books, as well as to encourage the publication of inexpensive editions to meet a popular demand for paperbacks. Another important decision was to recommend that a new book program be initiated to meet the needs in developing nations.

During the past decade the publication, sale, and format of books have gone through a complex and varied revolution. The population explosion, the spread of education, the war against illiteracy, and the increase in leisure time are contributing factors, as are the vast improvements in printing processes and methods of distribution. Along with newspapers, films, radio, and TV, books have become a vital part of mass communication phenomena. The emergence of the paperback has transformed not only techniques but also purposes of book publishers.

Through its publication system and libraries, which cover most areas of the world and speak to many national groups in a variety of tongues, UNESCO is a vast source of information. It literary function also deals with art, with beauty, with culture. Perhaps UNESCO's most vital contributions to international understanding and the building of world peace are the many volumes it produces and distributes which explain in plain language the common ideals and desires of peoples of various nations—the things of the mind and spirit which make for peace. In this sense bookmaking and book distribution are not neutral exercises; they are, rather, active factors—instruments—in the production of a world in which peace is a real possibility.

Questions for Discussion

1. How does the Universal Declaration of Human Rights support the right to an education?
2. To what extent is the government responsible for the education of the child?
3. What are some of the chief objectives of UNESCO?
4. Should private and parochial schools receive, directly or indirectly, government support?
5. What is the purpose of education?
6. Does every child have the right to a college education? What are the arguments for and against?
7. Where are children suffering for the lack of a proper education?
8. Why will it be more necessary than ever to have an education if and when computers "take over"—since computers can compile data but cannot make moral decisions?

Suggestions for Action

1. Read the preamble of the UNESCO Constitution.
2. Attend an open meeting of your local school board.
3. Visit a UNESCO documentation center.
4. It has been said that as individuals, we should live by

the standards we set for ourselves or find our souls destroyed by "moral erosion"—hypocrisy, cynicism, and despair. Make a special attempt to determine what "moral erosion" really is.

5. Form a panel discussion group; hold a public meeting on the issues presented in this chapter; get organizations connected with the UNA–USA to support the meeting.

6. Make a list of the values of a liberal education.

6. Food, Health, and the Population Explosion

Everyone has the right to a standard of living adequate for the health and well-being of himself and of his family, including food, clothing, housing and medical care and necessary social services, and the right to security in the event of unemployment, sickness, disability, widowhood, old age or other lack of livelihood in circumstances beyond his control.

—From the UN Universal Declaration of Human Rights

Hunger is a terrible taskmaster. It robs a person of his better self and it brings nations to the pit of starvation. Hunger has always been in the world; it has ranged from individual cases to the destruction of whole areas of civilization. Although the modern achievements of technology and science have made possible the production of more and better food and the saving of life, the sad fact is that through the population explosion now taking place—primarily in developing nations—the world is losing its fight against hunger.

"Hunger Is Unacceptable Morally and Socially"

Secretary-General U Thant quoted the Food and Agriculture Organization, "Hunger is unacceptable morally and socially; incompatible with the dignity of human beings; and a threat to social and international peace." He went on, "These are . . . merely *words* unless we can somehow understand that about half of the world's population goes to bed hungry every night. Probably the best way to understand this is not to think in terms of millions of hungry human beings, but of just one starving child. We have seen pictures of a starving child. Begin here. Then multiply this by a million and we will be somewhere near reality."

The Secretary-General, being realistic, proceeded to point out that during the UN Decade of Development, which has been established for the 1960's, the greatest task of the United Nations is to convince governments and peoples that they actually have the means to wipe out mass poverty with all its attendant miseries and dangers, and to encourage them to use these means to the full.

Now what is involved in this Decade of Development?

The chief purpose of the Decade of Development is to dramatize the fact that the gap in resources between the fully modernized nations and those nations still in the process of development is tending to widen, leaving about two thirds of humanity below the poverty line and turning developed societies (whether or not they fully realize it) into a privileged elite.

Therefore the Decade of Development is primarily a focus of action—of trying to close the gap by speeding up the processes of production; by releasing the majority of mankind from crippling poverty; by mitigating the tensions and hostilities which result from vast inequalities in wealth; and by restoring solidarity and hope.

The UN General Assembly has expressed the hope that "the flow of international assistance and capital should be increased substantially so that it might reach as soon as possible approximately one per cent of the combined national incomes of the economically advanced countries."

The launching of this Decade of Development represented a new departure in international economic relations. By agreeing to coordinate action, in order to attain a growth rate of 5 per cent in the developing nations, the United Nations extended the idea of expanding demand from a national to an international basis.

Although the idea was a good one, the actual practice has not met the established goals. In fact, during this very period the economy of the developing nations, instead of increasing, has declined. On the other hand, the economic growth of the advanced nations has overshot the mark. Thus the gap between the "haves" and the "have-nots" has widened. Because of this there are plans for an extension of the Decade of Development into the 1970–1980 period.

Freedom from Hunger Campaign

It has been pointed out that the twentieth century has witnessed three major revolutions:

1. *The political revolution.* It has given self-government to nearly a third of the world's population.
2. *The communications revolution.* It has broken down, through mass communication, the barriers of distance and language.
3. *The demographic revolution.* It has imparted to the whole challenge of want and poverty a new dimension.

It was against the background of these three world revolutions that the Food and Agriculture Organization created in 1960 the Freedom from Hunger Campaign. Its chief objectives are two: (1) to create a worldwide awareness of the problems of hunger and malnutrition which afflict more than half the world's population and which—apart from the human suffering and human degradation that is involved—pose a serious threat to world peace and orderly progress; and (2) to promote a climate of opinion in which solutions to these problems can be organized on both a national and an international basis.

The Freedom from Hunger Campaign, which has gained the support of international organizations, national governments, non-governmental organizations, and various citizens groups around the world, attempts to attack the problem of hunger on a broad front and at all levels of economic and social thought and action. It has three divisions of practical operation—information and education, research, and action.

The United Nations has issued three booklets dealing with various aspects of the campaign: "Population and Food Supply"; "Aspects of Economic Development"; and "National Development Efforts." Also, the Freedom from Hunger Campaign and the Decade of Development have been coordinated, and now supplement each other.

World Population: Challenge to Development

In 1800 the population of the world totaled less than one billion.

By 1920 it approached two billion.

In 1960 it was nearly three billion.

And by the year 2000, if present trends continue, it will probably reach six billion.

The population of the developing nations was increasing at unprecedented rates by the middle of the twentieth century. And unless the trends in fertility rates, over against mortality rates, are radically changed, the world is in for a self-made catastrophe of vast dimensions.

Dr. Eugene L. Smith, the U.S. Executive Secretary of the World Council of Churches, points up the total situation dramatically. He indicates that the major symbol of the cold war is no longer a line between East and West; rather it is a line circling the globe, roughly following the thirtieth parallel in the northern hemisphere—except that in Asia it swings north to follow Soviet Russia's border. This fateful line, Dr. Smith says, divides the world as follows:

North—a white majority
South—the colored majority of mankind

North—most of the major strongholds of the Christian faith
South—the major strongholds of non-Christian faiths

North—the most rapidly growing economies
South—the most rapidly growing populations

North—the massive concentration of prosperity
South—the massive concentration of poverty

Above the line are mainly white Christians; below the line, in the "have-not" areas, are mainly colored non-Christians. This fact must not be passed over lightly because embodied in it is not only the failure of Christianity in a moral and spiritual sense, but the possibility of a terrible struggle between communism and democracy.

That the religious community is at least aware of the problem of world poverty and economic development is indicated in the following statement issued by the International Affairs Commission of the National Council of the Churches of Christ in the U.S.A.:

World poverty, economic development, and justice. One priority of action is provided by the situation of world poverty. The broad facts are known: the rich are getting richer, the poor poorer; the rich north is white with a bad tradition of race relations, and the poor south is varicolored, the subject, directly or indirectly, of white injustice, the possessor of vivid memories and present experiences of racial oppression; the poor countries have been stirred by a vision of freedom and of plenty, a vision kept alive by partial—all too partial—achievement of these things. These facts have caused every informed and concerned person to issue warning after warning: this inequity, this injustice is brewing a human trouble that will dwarf our present difficulties.

Dalton F. McClelland, official representative at the UN for the World Alliance of YMCAs until his recent death, put it this way: "The greatest challenge, second to world peace, facing the world, the United Nations and its specialized agencies today, is whether the world's food supply can keep pace with the growth of population."

Understanding the Population Explosion

If anything realistic is to be done about the hunger problem there must be an understanding of what causes it and exactly where it is located. One must realize that the problem of hunger itself is not a new one; the present magnitude of the situation is new. Mankind has always had to be dependent upon the fluctuating seasons, productive and unproductive lands, rains and drought. This is very evident in the Bible, especially in the accounts of Joseph in Egypt. In fact, the balance between sufficiency and famine remained precarious throughout the world for centuries.

Moreover, as human inventions were developed in order to care for the needs of mankind, so the population grew. In some areas of the earth the population grew faster than the means to supply physical necessities. Then, of course, a process of depopulation set in through famine, disease, and war.

Through the centuries the population of the earth increased from a relatively few prototypes of man, to mankind moving upward—from tens or hundreds of thousands, century by century, to hundreds of millions at the beginning of the Christian era. At the time of the birth of Christ scholars estimate the total population of the earth to have been about two or three hundred million.

Since the early part of the nineteenth century revolutionary developments have occurred in the methods of producing the necessities of life, new methods of transportation have been developed, and medical science has cut the mortality rate drastically. Such terrible diseases as the plague, cholera, smallpox, and diphtheria have been virtually eliminated. This means that world population, instead of gaining and losing, is now on a steady and rapid upward scale. This also means that a fertility rate which only a few generations ago was essential to mere survival now results in a rapid multiplication of numbers (by reason of ever better control of mortality). For all through history only a fraction of all the babies born grew to maturity. Now, in the industrial nations of the West, only 5 per cent die before reaching adulthood. While an average of six to eight children per mother was once necessary to maintain human numbers, today only a fraction over two children per mother is necessary to maintain a stable population in the industrial countries. Even so, in these regions, which constitute about a quarter of the human race, the population growth is still very large in comparison with those of earlier epochs. For example, in the United States the prevailing rate of approximately three children per mother is only about half of what was considered a minimum in the traditional frontier society. Even this modest rate of reproduction —as compared with a century ago—increases the population at the rate of almost 50 per cent in a single generation.

But in the other sections of the earth, and particularly in the developing nations, relatively little control of fertility is practiced and families are large. What makes a serious situation is that in these areas—with persistently high birth rates and declining death rates, and with population growth already at an unprecedentedly high level—the rapid increase in population multiplies social and economic problems.

The population growth at the rates now observed in most of the underdeveloped nations is a major hindrance in solving the problems of food supply, as well as the general economic and social development of these needy areas. With only a few exceptions, the experts who have studied these conditions agree that the outlook would be far more favorable in these underdeveloped nations if the present rates of population increase could be slowed down by moderation of birth rates. The situation is growing so serious that some of these experts see little hope of improving conditions of life in these countries unless the birth rate is drastically reduced.

Birth Control and Increased Food Production: A "Both/And" Proposition

Experts are convinced that enough technical knowledge exists to meet the world's present food shortages and also to take care of the needs that will result from population growth for years to come. If everything possible were done to bring the existing technical knowledge of food production methods to bear fully throughout the world (and this would have to include large-scale programs of training key personnel; vigorous attacks on ignorance and inertia; and massive mobilization of capital on a worldwide scale of investments in agricultural and industrial development of the underdeveloped regions) then the food needs might be met. The fact of the matter is that such a mobilization of effort has not been possible and may not be possible.

The other side of the situation concerns population, or birth, control. Many experts believe that this is an imperative; that food production and birth control must go together. This lends force and urgency to the demands for policies in favor of birth regulation that are being pressed both on various governments and on the United Nations. But this is not so simple as it might seem, for some groups object to birth control in principle, or at least to certain forms of it. Others hold that the decision to practice it or not should be a purely personal matter without any governmental interference or pressure. The United Nations, faced with such sharp differences, has taken the position that the decision must be left up to each national government. The UN will assist governments if and when asked to do so. This is also the policy of the government of the United States; it will give birth control assistance when requested to do so by other governments.*

* A formal presentation to the United Nations of the World's Leaders' Declaration on Population, signed by the heads of thirty nations, was made at the UN on December 11, 1967, in connection with the commemoration of Human Rights Day (December

Several nations—India, Pakistan, mainland China, and Japan for example—have requested help in support of their national birth control projects. Assistance does not consist merely in helping to supply new and inexpensive birth control equipment, but also in educational and information services, clinics, and medical aid.

A long UN report on the total food and population problem concludes:

> Time is too precious to be wasted in futile arguments over what steps should be taken first to deal with the problem of population and food supply. Nothing less than an "all out" attack on all major aspects of the problem can bring success. To banish hunger and achieve a minimal diet for all people in the face of rapid population growth will at best take time. To check population growth in those countries where such is the desire of the people and their governments will also take time. And time is of the essence.

United Nations Agencies Now Serving

Although prior to World War II some international bodies were concerned with the promotion of health on a world scale, by the end of the war the need for a world organization was apparent. Therefore the agenda of the meeting which established the United Nations included an item pertaining to an international health organization. As a result of active support by Brazil and China, and then by other nations, the World Health Organization (WHO) was formed in 1948. The preamble of WHO's Constitution states:

"Health is a state of complete physical, mental and social well-being and not merely the absence of disease or infirmity."

In order to carry out its mandate WHO seeks the active assistance of governments, because most of its work consists of liaison—liaison between international organizations, between governments, between individual research workers and doctors throughout the whole field of medical and sociomedical science.

---

10). The signers declared, "We believe that the great majority of parents desire to have the knowledge and the means to plan their families; that the opportunity to decide the number and spacing of children is a basic human right."

As a specialized agency of the United Nations, WHO not only has developed new services but also has taken over many services that had already been begun before it came into existence. The core of WHO, as is the case of most other large agencies related to the UN, is the Secretariat. In the governing body, known as the World Health Assembly, three delegates from each member nation, plus a number of observers and advisers, discuss both the common problems with which WHO is directly concerned and technical problems of mutual interest. The program of work, presented by the Director-General and the Executive Board (which is made up of twenty-four specialists), constitutes the main "meat" of the Assembly agenda, and the actions taken become the program of the organization for the following year.

A large amount of cooperation exists in the area of health. The UN (in 1946) established the United Nations Children's Fund (UNICEF), which was originally devoted to efforts in assisting children in war-devastated areas, but since 1950 has shifted its emphasis to aid for long-range child programs in economically less-advanced nations. UNICEF works with WHO in the area of children's health. In recent years almost two thirds of UNICEF's budget has gone for material and child health programs and disease control campaigns (malaria, tuberculosis, yaws, leprosy, and trachoma).

Another specialized agency which works with WHO is the Food and Agriculture Organization (FAO). Naturally, in anything connected with nutrition the food experts of this agency are of great assistance. Both FAO and WHO have a number of special committees which work together on diseases that attack animals and men alike.

The International Labor Office also works with WHO in regard to everything concerning the health of workers.

Today, despite the immense advances made by medical science, disease takes a tremendous toll of life—greater than all those killed by accidents (including those on the highways) and by wars. Disease, however, is largely preventable, and the program of WHO assisted by the other specialized agencies mentioned above moves in this direction. Therefore its emphasis now is on health rather than on sickness. No other UN agency deals so directly with people as does WHO. This probably accounts for its ready acceptance by individuals as well as by the governments of the world.

Where Is the Driving Force?

In an editorial entitled "Business and the War on Hunger," *America* magazine (June 24, 1967) pointed out that even in selfish terms the war on hunger makes good business sense; but, it continued, many stockholders intent upon their next quarterly dividend do not seem to appreciate this. It quoted the chairman of a billion-dollar corn products company (in speaking to the First International Agri-business Conference) as saying,

> Where is the driving force for so massive an effort? For if there is to be a mobilization on a sufficient scale to conquer hunger, it must proceed from an unprecedented devotion to the highest expression of human values that any one of us can conceive—concern for the well-being of our fellow man. . . . World hunger will be dealt with effectively only when enough men recognize that it is a moral issue—and commit themselves to it.

Then *America* added: "Isn't that what Pope Paul in *Populorum Progressio,* and Pope John in *Mater et Magistra* and *Pacem in Terris,* together with numerous other religious leaders, have been telling us with growing urgency for some time?"

Questions for Discussion

1. Why is there a world food problem?
2. Can there ever be a proper balance between population growth and increased food production?
3. What does Pope Paul's encyclical *Populorum Progressio* say about population development?
4. What right has the United States government to distribute birth control information and devices both at home and abroad?
5. Where are the starvation areas of the world?
6. What must the nations of the world do in order to feed themselves properly?

Suggestions for Action

1. Make a special effort (in connection with a relief agency) to raise a fund for helping starving people.
2. Get up a petition urging Congress to increase its non-military foreign aid.
3. Write the mass media agencies (press, radio, and TV) urging more realistic presentations of the world population explosion and its consequences.
4. Form a panel discussion group; hold a public meeting on the issues presented in this chapter; get organizations connected with the UNA–USA to support the meeting.
5. Discover how valid is the contention that enough food can be raised to meet the demands of the growing population of the world.
6. Visit a planned parenthood clinic and find out what it does for the community in regard to birth control.
7. Look up the plan of Barbara Ward in relation to the rich nations aiding the poor nations.

7. Labor: Its Rights and Human Rights

> Everyone has the right to work, to free choice of employment, to just and favorable conditions of work and to protection against unemployment.
>
> Everyone, without any discrimination, has the right to equal pay for equal work.
>
> Everyone who works has the right to just and favorable remuneration insuring for himself and his family an existence worthy of human dignity, and supplemented, if necessary, by other means of social protection.
>
> Everyone has the right to form and to join trade unions for the protection of his interests.
>
> —From the UN Universal Declaration of Human Rights

In 1946 the International Labor Organization (ILO) became the first specialized agency associated with the United Nations. It had been established in 1919 as an autonomous institution connected to the League of Nations; its original constitution formed part of the Treaty of Versailles. All through the years it has made an outstanding contribution to the cause of human rights and fundamental freedoms.

In the preamble of ILO's constitution are found the basic principles which have led it to take leadership in the struggle for the rights of the people. It says:

> Universal and lasting peace can be established only if it is based upon social justice.
>
> Conditions of labor exist involving such injustice, hardship and privation to large numbers of people as to produce unrest so great that the peace and harmony of the world is imperilled . . .

The Implementation of Labor Rights

In order to implement the principles set forth in the preamble to its constitution ILO strengthened its purpose with the adoption of "The Declaration of Philadelphia" in 1944, which reads in part:

> . . . all human beings, irrespective of race, creed, or sex, have the right to pursue both their material well-being and their spiritual development in conditions of freedom and dignity, of economic security, and equal opportunity.

A distinctive feature of ILO is its tripartite structure: (1) It is an intergovernmental agency. (2) Employers and workers as well as governments participate in its work. (3) In ILO's democratic forum employers' and workers' delegates have a free voice.

The International Labor Conference is the supreme deliberative body of ILO. Its annual meeting in Geneva is attended by more than a thousand delegates, technical advisers, and observers. Each national delegation is composed of two government delegates, one employers' delegate, and one workers' delegate.

The Governing Body, which normally meets three or four times a year in Geneva, is composed of twenty government members, the employers' members, and the workers' members. This body elects the Director-General, approves the budget of ILO for adoption by the conference, determines policy and programs, and supervises the work of ILO and of its various committees and other bodies.

The International Labor Office, the organization's secretariat, research center, operational headquarters, and publishing house, occupies a large building on the banks of the Lake of Geneva. Staffed by some one thousand officials, representing eighty nationalities, it also has branch offices in several key locations around the world.

While these three organizations constitute ILO, it also acts through regional conferences, industrial committees, and other subsidiary bodies.

Chief among the functions of ILO is that of raising standards by building up a code of international law and practice by means of conventions and resolutions. Each convention is a legal instrument regulating some aspect of labor administration, social welfare, and human rights. When a convention is ratified by a nation, it has to report periodically to ILO on how the convention is being implemented.

International Labor Organization also operates extensively in the important area of technical cooperation. During recent years this has been carried out through the UN Special Fund. Under the expanded program of technical assistance such areas as health, education, agriculture, and social services are helped. International Labor Organization acts as the coordinator in cooperation with the United Nations, FAO, and UNESCO. Lately, steps have been taken to transfer executive responsibility for further implementation of programs to the authorities of the nations in which they are being developed, and also to make sure that these programs are within the framework of national economic development plans.

International Labor Organization also organizes technical meetings to deal with matters of concern to particular regions and industries. An International Institute for Labor Studies, established in Geneva, provides persons occupying positions of responsibility in the different nations with opportunities for advanced study of labor policy questions.

Among the many ILO projects are the following:

- The output in a "bottleneck" section of railway workshops in Burma was doubled.
- Production in a Nicaraguan shoe factory was boosted by 250 per cent.
- Power-loom weaving was tripled in Ceylon.

The work of ILO to improve productivity is part of a program that ranges all the way from development of rural industries to studies of the effects of automation; from protection of workers against radiation hazards to the promotion of labor-management cooperation and freedom of association.

Labor's Share in the International Covenants on Human Rights

From the point of view both of policy and of the implementation of basic labor principles the work of ILO bore fruit in the two international covenants adopted by the UN General Assembly on December 16, 1966. In these covenants are the essential concerns of labor developed through the years.

The International Covenant on Economic, Social, and Cultural Rights states in Part III, Article 6, that all nations which ratify the covenant recognize the right to work and safeguard this right; Article 7 recognizes the right of everyone to the enjoyment of just and favorable conditions of work. Article 8 recognizes the right of everyone to form trade unions and to join the trade union of his choice.

Article 10 indicates that special protection should be given to mothers during a reasonable period before and after childbirth; that during this time they should be accorded paid leave (or leave with adequate social security benefits). It provides also that children and young people should be protected from economic and social exploitation.

It is stated in Article 11 that everyone has the right to an adequate standard of living for himself and for his family.

The International Covenant on Civil and Political Rights (in Part III, Article 8) states that slavery and forced or compulsory labor are to be abolished, with certain exceptions made in recognition of national court rulings and during military conflict.

Labor's Share in the Decade of Development

The International Labor Organization is one of the UN-related agencies participating in the United Nations Development Program. Established November 22, 1965, the UNDP represents a consolidation of the Expanded Program of Technical Assistance and the Special Fund.

The Decade of Development, as related to concerns of labor, helps the low-income nations to develop by creating conditions that make capital investment feasible or more effective. It assists in surveys and feasibility studies to determine the potential (and to plan the use) of natural resources. It helps in establishing permanent educational institutions that can train large numbers of people in urgently needed skills. It aids in promoting applied research for the introduction of new techniques, the development of new products, and the improvement of productivity in agriculture and industry.

Projects assisted by the Decade of Development cover a wide range of activities: irrigation and cropping; forestry, fishing, and animal production; mining and manufacturing; power, transport, and communications; housing and building; trade and finance; health and sanitation; education from the primary to the university level; community development and industrial relations; and economic planning and public administration.

Already, as a result of these and other projects, more than 250,000 citizens of underdeveloped nations have received technical training in their own countries and over 30,000 others have acquired new skills through work and study fellowships abroad. Assistance is given through the assignment of internationally recruited experts who work in the area as well as the provision of equipment for training purposes, demonstrations, and pilot-scale projects.

The Worker Is a Man

Pope John XXIII declared in the encyclical *Mater et Magistra:*

> A worker is not merely a person to be engaged and paid for his work; he is a man, a member of human society, who helps to promote the advancement of that society by entering the industry in question.
>
> . . . Although it is in the interests of employers to treat their employees as human beings, they should look beyond purely utilitarian considerations, for productivity is not an end in itself.

Pope John carried this concept over into *Pacem in Terris.* It is reflected in the Pastoral Constitution on the Church in the Modern World of the Second Vatican Council, which in a real sense resulted from the hard work of this pope who has been honored by management and labor alike.

The encyclical on development (March 26, 1967) by Pope Paul VI is an excellent analysis and profound plea for aid to the developing nations. It points out labor's glory as well as some of its dehumanizing effects. On the one side, Pope Paul notes, "when work is done in common, when hope, hardship, ambition and joy are shared, it brings together and firmly unites the wills, minds and hearts of men: in its accomplishment, men find themselves to be brothers." On the other hand, under certain modern industrial and economic conditions, "there is a risk of its dehumanizing those who perform it, by making them its servants, for work is human only if it remains intelligent and free." *

Questions for Discussion

1. What rights does labor have?
2. Is not the labor movement taking advantage of its power of numbers?
3. Does every person have the right to work?
4. Why should workers have the right of collective bargaining?
5. When is a strike illegal?
6. Which system of government is better for the worker: capitalism or communism?
7. What makes labor organizations necessarily self-seeking?
8. How is the International Labor Organization helping to implement the Universal Declaration of Human Rights?

Suggestions for Action

1. Within the foundation stone of the International Labor Office in Geneva is a scroll which reads: "Sow Justice and Ye Shall Reap Peace." See if you can find a picture of this scroll.
2. Visit with a labor leader and get his ideas on the importance of collective bargaining.

---

* One of the best descriptions of the purpose and work of the International Labor Organization is to be found in the 66-page booklet published by the ILO office in Geneva, entitled *"The International Labor Organization."*

Since January 1, 1967, the UN Industrial Development Organization has been at work as an autonomous body within the United Nations to promote industrialization of developing nations and coordinate activities undertaken by the UN family in this area. Vienna is the permanent headquarters of UNIDO. Among its operational activities a program called Special Industrial Services (SIS) has been established. This program, which is financed from voluntary contributions, provides, on notice, assistance to nations wishing to promote or carry out new industrial projects. The second part of UNIDO's activities, that of studies and research, includes in particular the compilation, analysis, publication, and dissemination of data concerning various aspects of industrialization, such as industrial technology, investment, financing, production, management, and planning.

3. Secure a book from the public library depicting the advance of science during the past half-century. Note how this has changed day-by-day working conditions.

4. Form a panel discussion group; hold a public meeting on the issues presented in this chapter; get organizations connected with the UNA–USA to support the meeting.

5. Get a local labor leader to explain the moral and social aims of his organization.

6. Set up a group to play-act a strike, with one section acting out the position taken by management and the other the position taken by labor.

8. The Right to Self-Determination

Everyone is entitled to all the rights and freedoms set forth in this Declaration, without distinction of any kind, such as race, color, sex, language, religion, political or other opinion, national or social origin, property, birth or other status. Furthermore, no distinction shall be made on the basis of the political, jurisdictional or international status of the country or territory to which a person belongs, whether it be independent, trust, non-self-governing or under any other limitation of sovereignty.

—From the UN Universal Declaration of Human Rights

It is significant that both the International Covenant on Economic, Social, and Cultural Rights and the International Covenant on Civil and Political Rights (adopted simultaneously by the UN General Assembly on December 16, 1966) begin with an article on self-determination and the equal rights of people. This is not only an indication of how the principles of the UN Charter and the Universal Declaration of Human Rights are being implemented, but also a reflection of the notable emergence of newly independent nations since the Second World War.

A good illustration of this emergence of new nations is the number of flags of member nations that fly in front of the United Nations headquarters. In 1946 there were 51; in 1960 there were 97; in 1964 there were 115; and in 1968 there were 123. This means that the membership of the UN has more than doubled since its founding.

Pledged by its Charter to the principle of self-determination and the equal rights of all people, the UN has encouraged and assisted the rising national consciousness of the peoples of dependent territories and their determination to achieve independence. As Secretary-General U Thant has stated, "The United Nations stands for the self-government and independence of all people and the abolition of racial discrimination without reservations. It can never afford to compromise on these basic principles."

The UN and the Declaration on the Granting of Independence to Colonial Countries and Peoples

Under its charter (Chapters XII and XIII) the United Nations has established a system of trusteeship for territories placed under the system through individual agreements. The basic objective of this trusteeship system is to promote the political, economic, and social advancement of the trust territories and their progressive development toward self-government or independence. Most of the eleven territories placed under the trusteeship system have now gained their independence.

Besides the trusteeship system, administered by the UN Trusteeship Council, the charter lays down the principle of international responsibility for the welfare and advancement of independent peoples who have not yet gained a full measure of self-government (Chapter XI). Under this section of the charter, member nations of the UN, which have assumed responsibilities for the administration of non-self-governing territories, recognize the principle that the interests of the inhabitants of these territories are paramount and accept as a sacred trust the obligation to promote the well-being of the inhabitants. Moreover, they are to undertake the following: (1) to develop self-government, (2) to take due account of the political aspirations of the peoples, and (3) to assist them in the development of their free political institutions.

Taking this condition under consideration in a historic debate in 1960, the UN General Assembly expressed the desire for a speedy attainment of independence by such territories in a resolution entitled Declaration on the Granting of Independence to Colonial Countries and Peoples. In this declaration the conviction was expressed that the continued existence of colonialism prevented the development of international economic cooperation, that it impeded the social, cultural, and economic development of dependent peoples and that it militated against the United Nations' ideal of world peace.

On November 30, 1966, the UN General Assembly adopted a resolution which considered the consequences of the threat or the use of force in international relations and the right of peoples to self-determination.

Self-Determination and the Covenants on Human Rights

Despite the moral and political pressures of the Declaration on the Granting of Independence to Colonial Countries and Peoples, colonialism, some of a most degrading nature, has persisted in several areas of the world. Therefore, when the international covenants on human rights were finally completed and adopted by the UN General Assembly (1966), the implementation of the principles of the declaration had top priority.

Part I, Article 1, of the International Covenant on Economic, Social, and Cultural Rights states that "All peoples have the right of self-determination. By virtue of that right they freely determine their political status and freely pursue their economic, social, and cultural development."

In Part II, Article 2, paragraph 3 of the same document it is stated that "Developing countries, with due regard to human rights and their national economy, may determine to what extent they would guarantee the economic rights recognized in the present Covenant to non-nationals."

The implementation of self-determination is also given first place in the International Covenant on Civil and Political Rights. Part I, Article 1, repeats word for word three significant paragraphs found in the other covenant.

From Dependence to Freedom

The problems related to self-determination were brought to the surface in a seminar on human rights in developing countries held by the UN in Kabul, Afghanistan, May 12–25, 1964.*

One important problem discussed by the seminar was the matter of self-determination. Certain speakers stated that the right of all peoples to self-determination was of particular concern to developing countries, inasmuch as the majority of those countries had only recently emerged from a state of colonialism.

---

* The report of this seminar (forty-two pages) can be secured from the United Nations Office of Public Information.

On the matter of human rights there was general agreement that insofar as limitation of human rights was concerned the character of the administration of the developing countries should itself act in the spirit of the Universal Declaration of Human Rights and should accept responsibility for taking active measures to extend the enjoyment of human rights. The administration, it was said, should ensure that any legal limitations of those rights were clearly defined and that they reflected the spirit of the rights themselves.

In regard to genocide, one speaker drew attention to the broad definition of the "heinous crime" which was contained in the 1948 Convention on the Prevention and Punishment of the Crime of Genocide, adopted by the UN General Assembly. The convention, it was pointed out, condemned not only the physical destruction of religious, linguistic or national groups —or attempts to effect that destruction—but also practices tending to suppress the essential characteristics of such groups, such as the prohibition imposed upon alien members to teach or speak the language of the group, or to practice their religion (the so-called "cultural genocide"). The view was also expressed that intolerance and hatred, which might ultimately lead to genocide, were essentially due to ignorance and a poor sense of spiritual values among peoples. It is the duty of the nation itself, a speaker said, to educate the masses so as to give them a sense of respect for the creeds and customs of others. But unfortunately, it was pointed out, experience showed that certain acts of genocide had been committed either by governments themselves or by aggressive groups against which the government did not intervene.

One big factor in relation to self-determination is freedom of opinion and expression and freedom of information. In this seminar there was a general agreement that no distinction should be made between the developed and the developing nations in the recognition of the right of everyone to have freedom of opinion and expression as well as freedom of information.

Self-Determination Support From Other Bodies

Although the United Nations, as a result of its active concern for the liberation of peoples seeking self-determination, has become "the most potent vehicle for the channeling and focusing of this greatest revolution of our time: the setting of all humanity on the irreversible path of self-development" (the words of Dr. Charles H. Malik of Lebanon), other agencies outside the UN are working along with and in support of the United Nations in making sure that all people who want freedom will gain freedom—and all the human rights which go with freedom.

One such agency, the World Council of Churches, at its 1961 general assembly at New Delhi had much to say about human rights and the peoples around the world seeking independence.

Pope John XXIII said in *Pacem in Terris,*

> Even though there may be pronounced differences between political communities as regards the degree of their economic development and their military power, they are all very sensitive as regards their juridical equality and their moral dignity. For that reason, they are right in not easily yielding in obedience to an authority imposed by force, or to an authority in whose creation they had no part, or to which they themselves did not decide to submit by conscious and free choice.

The Pastoral Constitution on the Church in the Modern World, Vatican II (December 7, 1965), in its Section 2, "Building Up the International Community," has much to say about cooperation in "promoting the growth of developing nations."

In his challenging encyclical on Development of Peoples (March 26, 1967), Pope Paul VI said,

> The peoples themselves have the prime responsibility to work for their own development. But they will not bring this about in isolation. Regional agreements among weak nations for mutual support, more far-reaching agreements to establish programs for closer cooperation among groups of nations—these are the milestones on the road to development that leads to peace.

While great progress has been made in helping peoples gain their independence and in providing technical and other assistance to new nations, nevertheless, as the UN booklet "From

Dependence to Freedom" concludes, "Putting an end to colonialism and all practices of segregation and discrimination remains one of the most important goals to be achieved."

Questions for Discussion

1. Why should every nation have the right to self-determination?
2. What does the Universal Declaration of Human Rights say about the right of self-determination?
3. When is it impossible for a citizen to leave his country? What areas are barred to United States citizens?
4. Why should every person have the right to change his religion, political party, or residence?
5. Where are the slave camps today?
6. Who determines the destiny of people in a democracy? In a dictatorship?
7. How can we ever achieve a system of government that will encourage self-determination?
8. What is meant by "trust territory"?

Suggestions for Action

1. Attend a session at the UN dealing with trust territories.
2. Look up the meaning of *apartheid* in a modern dictionary; write it down.
3. Visit UN headquarters when the flags are flying and note the number of new member nations.
4. Form a panel discussion group; hold a public meeting on the issues presented in this chapter; get organizations connected with the UNA–USA to support the meeting.
5. Invite a UN delegate from a newly formed nation to speak at some meeting in your community.
6. Make a list of all the nations that have come into being within the past ten years.

9. Refugees and Their Rights

Everyone has the right to leave any country, including his own, and to return to his country.

Everyone has the right to seek and to enjoy in other countries asylum from persecution.

—From the UN Universal Declaration of Human Rights

Although the refugee problem is of long standing, the 1967 war in the Middle East has increased it to an alarming extent. This, in addition to a critical refugee situation in Africa, has taxed the United Nations beyond capacity, and the time has come for a greatly increased cooperative effort on the part of the UN, denominational relief agencies, and other voluntary groups to meet adequately the challenge of this new crisis. Not only are food, shelter, clothing, and spiritual aid needed, but also at the bottom of the refugee situation is the political problem of many involved nations. Along with emergency aid must go a serious consideration of how to solve the international, long-term refugee problem.

The Convention Relating to the Status of Refugees

The most important document adopted for the benefit of refugees is the 1951 Convention Relating to the Status of Refugees. It sets out and codifies the minimum rights of the refugees. These include such items as freedom of religion, access to courts, the right to work and to education, and the right to social security.

The convention ensures that the contracting nations shall not expel a refugee on their territory except on the grounds of national security or public order, and that no refugee shall be expelled or returned in any manner whatsoever to the frontiers of territories where his life or freedom would be threatened on account of his race, religion, nationality, membership in a particular social group, or political opinion.

It also provides for the issuance of travel documents to

refugees and makes special reference to the problem of refugee seamen, who, serving as crew members on board merchant ships and owing to lack of documents permitting them to return to any country, have been unable to set foot on shore legally. (An agreement concluded by eight maritime nations at The Hague, November, 1957, provides for measures that have enabled thousands of these seamen to regularize their position.)

Work of the Refugee Office

At first (in 1951) an estimated 1,250,000 refugees came under the general mandate of the United Nations. Of these about 400,000 were non-settled and needed some form of assistance. Most of these were in Displaced Persons Camps in Europe. But by January, 1963, the number of these DPs, primarily in Europe, had been reduced to 45,000, of whom 41,000 were still living in camps in Austria, Germany, Greece, and Italy.

Thus by 1962 the UN High Commissioner's Office for Refugees had reached an important stage in its history, and, as far as material assistance programs were concerned, three main tasks remained to be performed:

1. to complete the last major programs for the so-called "old refugees" in Europe;
2. to ensure that the unsettled refugees do not gradually re-form into a dense mass with all the accompanying distress and bitterness possible;*
3. to tackle new refugee problems in Africa and other areas such as Hong Kong, Cambodia, and Spain (Cuban refugees).

Refugees, as defined by a UNHCR statute, are persons who, owing to well-founded fear of persecution for reasons of race, religion, nationality, or political opinion, are outside their country of origin and cannot avail themselves of the protection of that country or, owing to such fear, do not wish to. (Thousands fleeing from the Soviet Union into Germany after World War II is a good example of this.)

*It should be kept in mind that the Palestine refugee situation —which did develop these characteristics—was under a different UN agency. This situation will be dealt with later in this chapter.

In meeting the refugee situations mainly outside of Europe the United Nations office acts under the directives of the General Assembly. Here it makes its "good offices" available to governments.

The chief role of the United Nations refugee office is to be an initiator and catalyst, bringing together and making use of all available energies and resources of governments and of voluntary agencies, and keeping in touch with the technical assistance services and specialized agencies of the UN in order, whenever possible, to secure their help in meeting the variety of refugee situations.

As a result of such services the UN High Commissioner's Office for Refugees was awarded the Nobel Peace Prize in 1954.

New Refugee Demands

The UN 1967 report covering the refugee situation noted that Africa is drawing the heaviest on the UN High Commissioner's Office for Refugees. Of 170,000 new refugees, as of 1966, 125,000 were in Africa. And although this UN agency, according to its mandate, is called upon to help refugees in all parts of the world—notably Asia, Europe, and Latin America —$2,000,000 out of its financial goal of $4,200,000 went for African refugees.

There are approximately 740,000 refugees in Africa. On that continent the march of history has been advancing at a rapid rate during the past few years. At times the creation of new nations has been noisy and dangerous. In their quest for independence young Africans especially have been willing to bear arms, resulting in rebellions and uprisings of many kinds. Political differences are involved, as are clashes between different social and tribal groups. As a result, people have been forced out of one territory into another against their will. It is a situation, from a human point of view, similar to what happened in Europe after World War II and in the Middle East after the Israeli-Arab conflicts of 1948 and 1967.

This means that such agencies as the International Labor Organization, the World Health Organization, UNESCO, the Food and Agricultural Organization, and the UN Development Program will have to help the UN refugee agencies with the problem. And, besides, the funds in much larger amounts will have to come from both governments and private agencies. Such funds are needed to consolidate settlements already established for Rivandese in Burundi, Democratic Republic of the Congo, United Republic of Tanzania and Uganda; for refugees from Portuguese Guinea in Senegal; for refugees from Angola in the Congo; and Mozambiquans in South-East Tanzania and Sudanese in Uganda.

Besides emergency "housing," food, and medical care, various educational systems, supported by voluntary funds, have been established.

The Rights of Refugees

Albert F. Bender, Jr., UN Deputy High Commissioner for Refugees, speaking before a meeting of non-governmental organizations interested in the International Year for Human Rights at the *Palais des Nations,* Geneva, on December 9, 1966, stressed the importance of the article in the Universal Declaration of Human Rights which reads: "Everyone has the right to seek and to enjoy in other countries asylum from persecution."

Mr. Bender then went on to outline the steps which the Commission on Human Rights and Committee III of the UN General Assembly had taken to implement this article by a series of recommendations leading up to a draft declaration. He said that "once achieved, such a formal expression, having the full moral weight of the General Assembly behind it, will represent a most positive development, for, as far as the refugee is concerned, the granting of asylum is the condition precedent for the enjoyment of almost all other human rights." He then proceeded to emphasize the importance of a new protocol eliminating the 1951 date.

A "Protocol" Adopted to Cover New Refugees

On January 31, 1967, the President of the General Assembly (at that time Abdul Rahman Pazhwak of Afghanistan) and the Secretary-General of the United Nations, U Thant, signed a copy of an international instrument designed to extend to new groups of refugees the legal position of persons covered by the 1951 Convention Relating to the Status of Refugees. Known as the "Protocol," it removed in effect the January 1, 1951, deadline and also what Prince Sadruddin Aga Khan, UN High Commissioner for Refugees, called "a particularly regrettable discrimination as between different groups of refugees, especially with regard to African refugees."

The "Protocol" notes that the 1951 convention on refugees covers only those persons who became refugees as a result of events prior to January, 1951. Yet new refugee situations have arisen since 1951, which would not be legally covered by the convention. Now, with the additional "Protocol" all refugees will have equal treatment under the international agreements.

The Refugee Support Given by the United States

Ambassador Patricia R. Harris, United States Representative on UN Committee III, in reporting on how her government had supported the refugee situation, and how it would continue to do so, said:

> . . . Our role in assisting refugees since World War II has been exerted principally through: (1) a series of special immigration acts and administrative measures which have enabled 1.2 million refugees to find new homes in the United States, most of them as citizens; the most recent legislation in this field was the Congressional authorization under the revised Immigration and Nationality Act for the entry of up to 10,200 refugees each year; (2) direct programs throughout the world involving expenditures of over $1.2 billion; and (3) our participation in the United Nations and in other intergovernmental programs, involving U.S. contributions of $850 million.
>
> In 1966 $115 million is being spent by the United States on refugee programs supported by our government directly or through multilateral aid. Over $1 billion has been contributed since World War II by the American people to the cause of refugees through private non-governmental institutions. . . .
>
> The United States pledges its continued strong support to the High Commissioner in his discharge of his vital task.

UN Refugee Program in the Middle East

As an aftermath of the 1948 Israeli-Arab hostilities in Palestine, hundreds of thousands of Palestinian Arabs became refugees—losing their homes, possessions, and livelihoods. After a period of emergency assistance channeled through voluntary agencies, the UN General Assembly in December, 1949, established the United Nations Relief and Works Agency for Palestine Refugees in the Near East (UNRWA) to assist these refugees.*

This refugee organization is of a special nonpolitical and "temporary" nature. It cooperates with the so-called "host governments" (which have been Jordan, Lebanon, the Syrian Arab Republic, and the United Arab Republic). It provides basic rations, health and welfare services, and shelter for the refugees, along with education and training. Over a million refugees have been registered with the agency; now, with the 1967 war, the number has increased greatly.

This UN refugee program has aimed to increase assistance to the maturing refugees in order to enable them to develop their innate talents. Funds have been devoted to expanding facilities for vocational training, increasing the number of university scholarships, and making rather modest yet essential improvements in the general educational program.

Due to the fact that 50 per cent of these refugees in the Middle East are below the age of eighteen, UNRWA's educational program—which is run in cooperation with UNESCO—is an important phase of its work. It offers six years of elementary education to all refugee children, and preparatory and secondary education to an ever-increasing number of the young refugees.

The income of UNRWA has been provided by voluntary contributions, largely from governments. Non-governmental

---

* The reader seeking a complete account of the UNRWA program is referred to a booklet, "UNRWA 1967," and a leaflet, "UNRWA and the Palestine Refugees," which can be secured from the United Nations Office of Public Information.

Prince Sadruddin Aga Khan, UN High Commissioner for Refugees, in reporting to the UN General Assembly on November 22, 1967, pointed out that "the events in the Near East have resulted in a recrudescence of refugee arrivals in Europe."

and private contributions have also played an important part, particularly in the agency's vocational training scholarship program, under which donors can finance scholarships for individual refugees. The agency, however, has been faced with an increasingly critical financial situation. The UNRWA Commissioner-General has appealed to governments, to voluntary organizations, and to individuals for additional contributions. Now, with a greatly enlarged responsibility due to the increased number of refugees created by the 1967 conflict, millions of additional dollars must be made available to Arab refugees (and, to a less degree, Israeli refugees) who have become the innocent victims of an international strife with terrible national bitterness and religious overtones. And unless the refugee situation can somehow be resolved it will continue to plague the entire complex political problem.

Before hostilities broke out in the Middle East on June 5, 1967, the United Nations Relief and Works Agency had fifty-four refugee camps in Syria, Jordan, Lebanon, and the Gaza Strip. About six thousand local employees and eighty international supervisors took part in the provision of food, medical services, education, and other help for refugees. In the camps were not only hundreds of thousands of Arabs who fled Israel at the outbreak of the 1948 conflict, but a whole new generation of refugees, born and educated in the camps, knowing no other home. This conflict left in its wake some 800,000, a figure which grew to an estimated 1,300,000 even before the 1967 war.

Non-Governmental and Religious Refugee Agencies

Besides the United Nations refugee program, but in cooperation with it, are those of several secular and religious relief agencies, which provide millions of dollars annually in food, clothing, medical supplies, and personnel. Much of this work is done on an interfaith basis.

The National Council of Churches carries on much of its refugee work in close cooperation with the Division of Inter-Church Aid, Refugee and World Service of the World Council of Churches, whose headquarters are in Geneva. Also, with headquarters in the same city, is the World Alliance of Young Men's Christian Associations, which has rendered an outstanding service through the years both to refugees and to prisoners of war. In 1964 the UNRWA *Newsletter*, "Palestine Refugees Today," was dedicated to the World Alliance of YMCAs "whose invaluable participation has done so much to make the (UNRWA) program a beneficial force in the life of the refugee community."

The YMCA and Refugees

At the April 10–11, 1967, meeting of the Standing Committee on Work with Refugees and Migrants of the World Alliance of YMCAs, held in Geneva, it was reported that in 1966 the number of refugees increased by one and a half million and that the need for YMCA services had become greater than ever. It was then reported that for 1968 there would have to be a continuation of YMCA refugee services in Hong Kong, India, Pakistan, Gaza, Jordan, Lebanon, Austria, France (and those carried on by the Polish YMCA in England and France); an intensification of work in Vietnam and Tanzania; and an extension of YMCA refugee services to Uganda and Zambia.

In a memorandum the World Alliance of YMCAs pointed out that an estimated 1,678,000 are refugee/displaced persons in Vietnam, out of a total population of 16,500,000. Of these, some 540,000 have been resettled, about 400,000 have been given temporary shelters in camps and the rest are living out of camps. The Vietnamese refugees are typical farm families driven from their land. Most of them are women and children. They live in overcrowded quarters, under unsanitary conditions. "They have no land to farm, no work to do, so they spend their time in aimless wandering about and live in apathy and frustration from day to day."

The YWCA Program

The YWCA of the U.S.A., by means of funds contributed through the World YWCA, helps make possible services to refugees in various parts of the world. The programs are varied, but work with women and children, vocational training, and child care are special emphases.

The most recent among such efforts is taking place in Vietnam, where a YWCA staff member is working; others are being recruited from Southeast Asia to cooperate with the East Asia Christian Service, particularly in group work with displaced women and children.

The services to Palestinian refugees in Jordan have been continuously in operation in the Aqabat Jaber Camp and in Amman and Jerusalem, with the Jordanian and the World YWCAs working together. Currently, the YWCAs in that region are concentrating on work in the new refugee camps on the East Bank of Jordan.

In Pakistan the YWCA has played a distinctive role in the process of integration of the former inhabitants of camps into new housing areas. The YWCA has moved with the people to the new areas, where it is continuing its community services and helping them to put down new roots.

In Hong Kong the YWCA is extending its services into the crowded settlements, offering social and educational activities to refugees. Nurseries and play centers for small children—some of them on rooftops of resettlement blocks—are being operated by the Hong Kong association.*

More Than "Refugees"

Prince Sadruddin Aga Khan, the UN High Commissioner for Refugees, in giving his 1966 report stressed the fact that refugees are human beings and must, as soon as possible, be returned to their full status as citizens. "It can never be overemphasized," he said, "that to keep refugees in refugee transit centers—I refuse to call these centers 'camps'—indefinitely, is the very negation both of the spirit and of the letter of the 1951 convention. The granting of asylum, in my opinion, cannot be regarded as an end in itself."

He went on to explain, "This means, in the *first place,* that the States granting asylum must certainly, in their own interests, in the interest of peace and stability and in the interest of the international community generally, do all they can to integrate those of the refugees who desire integration; and in the *second place* that the countries able to receive those who have been unable or unwilling to remain in the country of first asylum should keep their doors wide open for these refu-

* Church World Service also has an extensive program among refugees in Hong Kong.

gees, raising their quotas when necessary and continuing to apply increasingly flexible admission criteria." This the United States has been doing, much to its credit.*

Questions for Discussion

1. Where are the most acute refugee areas at the present time?
2. What is the UN (through its various relief agencies) doing to help the refugee situation?
3. Why cannot the Arabs and Israelis settle their own refugee problems?
4. What has turned Africa into the most acute refugee area?
5. Why is there a refugee problem in South Vietnam?
6. What is organized religion doing about the refugee situation?
7. Where have resettled refugees made a major contribution toward the development of their new home areas?

Suggestions for Action

1. Visit, if possible, a refugee camp. Or show a movie of life in a refugee camp.
2. Have a representative of Church World Service, or some other refugee resettlement organization, come and give a report on the current refugee situation.
3. Contact a refugee family and find out if it would like any special help.
4. Form a panel discussion group; hold a public meeting

* Reporting to the UN Economic and Social Council at Geneva on August 1, 1967, Prince Aga Khan said that of the 740,000 refugees in Africa at the beginning of 1967, 450,000 could be considered settled (350,000 largely through spontaneous integration after initial outside aid, and 100,000 mainly as a result of international assistance). Although progress in 1966 had been on the whole favorable, he expressed concern over the fact that, for 1967, governments had so far contributed only $3,000,000 towards the financial goal of $4,800,000. "It is solely due to private contributions from a number of voluntary organizations participating in the great European Refugee Campaign which took place last fall that we still hope to find a way to carry through this year's programs," he declared.

on the issues presented in this chapter; get organizations connected with the UNA–USA to support the meeting.

5. Discover why the UN is not caring for the refugees in South Vietnam.

6. Pack and send through a refugee agency a box of good used clothing for use in a refugee camp.

10. International Law and Its Benefits

Everyone charged with a penal offence has the right to be presumed innocent until proved guilty according to law in a public trial at which he has had all guarantees necessary for his defence.

No one shall be held guilty of any penal offence on account of any act or omission which did not constitute a penal offence, under national or international law, at the time when it was committed. Nor shall a heavier penalty be imposed than the one that was applicable at the time the penal offence was committed.

No one shall be subjected to arbitrary interference with his privacy, family, home or correspondence, nor to attacks upon his honor and reputation. Everyone has the right to the protection of the law against such interference or attacks.

—From the UN Universal Declaration of Human Rights

Just as a nation has to have law and order to survive and to function properly, so does the international community. This is especially true with regard to international peace. It is also essential in the areas of human rights and fundamental freedoms. Basic principles are not enough; they need the support of international law. Injustice, if it cannot be controlled by compassion, must be confronted by law.

As we have noted in the previous chapter, a worldwide code of law has gradually been constructed through the years, primarily by the UN Commission on Human Rights, the UN Commission on the Status of Women, and two specialized agencies, the International Labor Organization (ILO) and the UN Educational, Scientific, and Cultural Organization (UNESCO). They have developed a number of international conventions, each protecting a particular right. Each, when ratified, enters into force and is legally binding on the ratifying nations. Quite appropriately, the first UN convention deals with the first of all human rights—the right to life itself. At the very session where the Universal Declaration of Human

Rights was proclaimed the UN General Assembly adopted unanimously the Genocide Convention, which declares that genocide is a crime under international law. (The United States has not yet ratified it or any other of the United Nations conventions.)

The International Court of Justice

One of the principal purposes of the United Nations is "to bring about by peaceful means, and in conformity with the principles of justice and international law, adjustment or settlement of international disputes or situations which might lead to a breach of the peace." It was with this objective in view that the UN Charter created the International Court of Justice as one of the chief organs of the United Nations.

The International Court of Justice, located at The Hague in the Netherlands, is the UN's legal instrument. It seeks (as the UN Charter puts it) "conditions under which justice and respect for obligations arising from treaties and other sources of international law can be maintained." Representing the hope that some day there will be a world of law which will govern the relations of one nation with another, the court now has the power to settle disputes on any matter brought before it by two or more nations. It has the power to interpret an international treaty, but it does not have the power to enforce its decisions, although an appeal can be made to the UN Security Council.

The UN Charter, legally, is an instrument of international law. When nations become UN members, they are under solemn obligation to abide by its principles and purposes. For many of the newly independent countries, this may be their first introduction to international cooperation under law. But for many of the older governments, the UN Charter is a constant reminder of their obligations to their fellow UN members. Hardly a day goes by, when the UN is in session, without one nation or another being reminded of its responsibility under the Charter.

Moreover, one of the chief purposes of the Security Council is to get nations into the habit of using just and peaceful means of settling their quarrels. The UN General Assembly also plays its part in developing a nation's sense of international responsibility by seating it in dignity and equality with every other nation, whether large or small. Article 36 of the Charter indicates that the Security Council, when called upon to make recommendations in a dispute—the continuance of which is likely to endanger the maintenance of international peace and security—should take into consideration that legal disputes as a general rule be referred by the parties to the International Court of Justice.

Judges of the court are elected for terms of nine years and are eligible for re-election. Every three years it elects its President and Vice-President, who are also eligible for re-election. The judges are bound to hold themselves permanently at the disposal of the court, unless they are on leave or are prevented by illness or other serious reasons recognized as valid. No judge of the court may exercise any political or administrative function or engage in any act as agent, counsel, or advocate in any suit, or participate in the decision of any case in which he has previously taken part as a representative of one of the parties (or in any other capacity).

As a protection against political pressure, it is provided that no judge can be dismissed unless, in the unanimous opinion of the other judges, he has ceased to fulfill the required conditions. When engaged in the business of the court, the judges enjoy diplomatic privileges and immunities. And before taking up their duties, they must take a solemn declaration in open court that they will exercise their powers "impartially and conscientiously."

The court, apart from its jurisdiction to deal with contentious cases, also has the power to give advisory opinions—that is, its views on any legal question at the request of the UN General Assembly, the Security Council, or other UN bodies authorized to do so. It is open to nations that are not parties to its Statute (on conditions laid down by a Security Council resolution of October 15, 1946). It is not open to private individuals. No nation is forced to submit cases to the court, since the UN Charter provides that members of the UN may entrust the solution of their differences to other tribunals.

At this point it is interesting to note that the National Council of Churches, meeting in San Francisco in 1960, declared,

> As a significant step toward world law for a world community, the United States should uphold and strengthen the

International Court of Justice. Our nation should abrogate self-appointed power to deny to the Court its legitimate jurisdiction. In this and other ways, encouragement should be given to increasing the rule of law for developing a community of nations.

The Legal Aspects of Human Rights Conventions

A convention, in international law, is an agreement among sovereign nations. It is a legal compact which pledges every contracting party to accept certain obligations. In other words, it is a treaty among nations.

Four human rights conventions are now before the U.S. Senate Foreign Relations Committee:

1. The Convention on the Prevention and Punishment of the Crime of Genocide;
2. The Convention on the Political Rights of Women;
3. The Supplementary Convention on the Abolition of Slavery, the Slave Trade and the Institutions and Practices Similar to Slavery;
4. The Convention Concerning the Abolition of Forced Labor.

The issue of U.S.A. ratification caused the New Jersey Bar Association to study the subject of the human rights conventions. Its Special Committee on International and Comparative Law and World Organization reported that ratification of the conventions had been approved by several state bar associations, by the Committee on International Law of the Association of the Bar of the City of New York, and by several other non-legal organizations within the nation.

After reviewing the purpose and contents of each of the conventions it considered in detail their constitutionality. It pointed out that the question of ratification of any treaty has in it two limitations on the treaty-making power of the United States government: (1) that no treaty may be entered into which contravenes the prohibitions against federal action contained in the United States Constitution, and (2) that treaties must deal with matters of "international concern." The committee reported that it "is satisfied, from a reading of the Conventions, that they do not violate any prohibition against federal action, and that they are properly matters of 'international concern.' "

In view of these findings the committee adopted the following resolution:

> Our recommendation to support the ratification of these Conventions is based on moral grounds which should be legally implemented. We, as civilized members of society, abhor the practices which the Human Rights Conventions are designed to eliminate. We must, therefore, put our weight behind the efforts of those who seek to have abuses of human beings eliminated wherever such abuses may occur.

Bruno V. Bitker, testifying before the Senate Foreign Relations Committee as Chairman of the Committee on Human Rights of the United States National Commission for UNESCO, declared:

> By its heritage and its ideals, because of its good will toward all mankind and its desire for peace throughout the world, the United States has assumed international responsibilities. It now has the opportunity and the obligation to vigorously continue to advance the cause of human rights and fundamental freedoms everywhere on earth. To further this noble objective, we should speedily ratify the pending four human rights treaties on Genocide, on Slavery, on Forced Labor and on the Political Rights of Women.

Scores of Other Nations, but Not the United States

Legal ratification of human rights conventions is what we are primarily concerned about in this chapter. Here the *legal* aspects are being stressed and this section should therefore be considered in relation to the first chapter, which deals with the conventions and their general implementation.

As was pointed out by the testimony submitted on March 8, 1967, to the Senate Foreign Relations Committee by a number of Jewish organizations which comprise the National Community Relations Advisory Council, as of November 1, 1966, seventy-five nations had ratified the Forced Labor Convention; sixty-seven the Slavery Convention; fifty the Political Rights of Women Convention; and seventy the Genocide Convention.

At the close of the document (with the notation "Of Counsel: Phil Baum, William B. Korey, Sidney Liskofsky") are these words:

> To sum up therefore: If no constitutional problem exists, if the provisions of the treaties are fully consonant with domestic law, and if the issue is fundamentally one of policy, then the conclusion is self-evident. Policy considerations involving our foreign relations, and fully elaborated upon earlier, demand that our nation end its self-imposed abstinence from creative undertakings in the field of international human rights and restore to ourselves a leading role in extending the rule of law throughout the globe. We earnestly hope that this Committee will recommend that the Senate consent to ratification of the conventions on slavery, forced labor, political rights of women and genocide, and therewith provide—in the words of Ambassador Goldberg—"a tremendous impetus" . . . for the world-wide battle for human rights.

A Great Step Forward

The unanimous adoption of the International Covenants on Human Rights by the UN General Assembly on December 16, 1966, represented a great victory for the Commission on Human Rights, for this event was the successful culmination of the commission's eighteen years of work in attempting to undergird the Universal Declaration of Human Rights with a firm legal foundation.

When the Commission on Human Rights began this work in 1947, and as the texts were developed in detail in conjunction with the Economic and Social Council and the Third (Social, Humanitarian, and Cultural) Committee of the UN General Assembly, several questions arose. Should there be one or two covenants, that is, should civil and political rights, on the one hand, and economic, social, and cultural rights, on the other, be regulated in a single convention or in two separate treaties? Should the covenants contain an article on the right of peoples and nations to self-determination?

The view prevailed, after long discussion, that there should be two separate covenants because civil and political rights could be secured immediately, but adequate economic, social, and cultural rights could be achieved only progressively according to each nation's available resources. The two covenants, however, contain a large number of similar provisions, and were opened for signature simultaneously.

It should be noted in this chapter especially that there are two distinct sets of implementation measures in the covenants.

Nations ratifying, for example, the Covenant on Civil and Political Rights will elect a Human Rights Committee, composed of eighteen persons acting in an individual capacity. This committee will consider reports submitted by the "states parties" and may address general comments to these nations, as well as to the Economic and Social Council. Moreover, under the Optional Protocol (which will come into force only when ten nations have accepted it) the Human Rights Committee may also consider communications from private individuals claiming to be the victims of a violation by a "state party" to the protocol of any of the rights set forth in the covenant.

Nations ratifying the Covenant on Economic, Social, and Cultural Rights undertake to submit periodic reports to the Economic and Social Council on the measures adopted and the progress made toward the realization of these rights. Then the council, upon consideration of the reports, and in cooperation with other UN bodies and the specialized agencies, may promote appropriate international action to assist the "states parties" in those fields.

Thus we have here in these two covenants (or treaties), for the first time in history, international protection for the rights of man, for these covenants in due course will become legally binding on those nations which ratify them. As stated in the *UN Monthly Chronicle*, "Their approval by the Assembly represents a milestone in United Nations efforts to win universal recognition and respect for human rights."

Implementation Through International Law

Human rights are so basic to world peace that it is no longer enough to state them as principles to be considered; now they are considered so essential that they must be implemented by means of international law. This is well illustrated by what transpired at the meeting of the UN Commission on Human Rights in Geneva, in March, 1967.

At the observance of the first International Day for the Elimination of All Forms of Racial Discrimination, held in the Assembly Hall of the *Palais des Nations,* the chairman recalled that March 21 commemorated the seventh anniversary of the Sharpeville massacre in South Africa, when peaceful demonstrators against racial discrimination had been fired upon and killed by the authorities. Declaring that racial discrimination was the "most flagrant and widespread violation of human rights in the modern world," he said that the struggle against this evil concerned all mankind.

He added that the United Nations had a duty to bring about the elimination of all forms of racial discrimination, and mentioned the fact that the UN General Assembly had adopted various instruments and resolutions in the area of human rights. Now the time has come, he emphasized, *for active steps to give effect to the principles and standards of international law, and the decisions and appeals of the United Nations, so that with the help of all men of goodwill, every human being would one day be able to enjoy the material and spiritual blessings of life.**

* At its twentieth session, the UN General Assembly launched a new program "to promote the teaching, study, dissemination and wider appreciation of international law." The Secretary-General, in conjunction with UNESCO, will initiate and carry out this program. Success of this venture, it is pointed out, will depend upon active support from member nations, national and international institutions, and individual scholars and lawyers.

On July 18, 1966, the International Law Commission completed its final text of seventy-five draft articles on the law of treaties and decided to recommend to the UN General Assembly the convening of a diplomatic conference to study the draft articles and to conclude a convention on the law of treaties. This recommendation was endorsed by the General Assembly at its twenty-first session, when it adopted a resolution requesting the Secretary-General to convoke such a conference in two sessions, in 1968 and in 1969.

On December 17, 1966, the UN General Assembly adopted a resolution by which it decided to establish a United Nations Commission on International Trade Law "which shall have for its object the promotion of the progressive harmonization and unification of the law of international trade."

Questions for Discussion

1. How does the International Court of Justice operate?
2. What related organization in the UN is developing protection by law? Explain.
3. Can a person avoid arbitrary arrest? In what ways?
4. How can a person always get a fair trial?
5. In what ways can a person be protected against unfair fines and penalties?
6. Who is to determine when a person is guilty or not?
7. Why is it necessary to keep making new laws?
8. How does international law differ from that of a state or nation?

Suggestions for Action

1. Call upon a lawyer and ask him what rights a person has to protect himself from being placed, and held, in a mental institution.
2. Find out from your Congressman why the Universal Declaration of Human Rights does not have the status of law.
3. Form a human rights seminar in your community with a topic dealing with the functions of the International Court of Justice and world peace.
4. Visit a court of law while it is in session and see how the law operates.
5. Make a chart or diagram showing, stage by stage, how a person accused of a crime has the protection of the law.
6. Get a lawyer to explain the basic differences between the various law courts of our nation and the process of international law.

11. A Day, a Week, and a Year for Human Rights

Everyone has the right freely to participate in the cultural life of the community, to enjoy the arts and to share in scientific advancement and its benefits.
—From the UN Universal Declaration of Human Rights

The main purpose of this chapter is to provide a practical guide for voluntary organizations that want to promote the interests of the United Nations and, in particular, to implement those basic aspects of the Universal Declaration of Human Rights that have been dealt with in the preceding chapters. Publicity tools and public relations techniques will therefore be related directly to the substance of this material so that it may have expression in local communities. In order to make this public relations process relevant, specific ways in which to promote Human Rights Day and the International Year for Human Rights are presented in some detail.

Human Rights Day

As Secretary-General U Thant has said, "In the philosophy of the United Nations, respect for human rights is one of the main foundations for freedom, justice and peace in the world. Hence the celebration of Human Rights Day on December 10 has a profound meaning for all people everywhere." Human Rights Day marks the anniversary of the formal adoption of the Universal Declaration of Human Rights by the UN General Assembly on December 10, 1948.

As has been noted throughout this book, the Universal Declaration of Human Rights is one of the great documents of modern times and therefore deserves a special annual commemoration. We celebrate this day because the adoption of the Declaration represents the culmination of an intensive effort by several bodies of the United Nations to give expression to the will of mankind: a common standard of achievement in the recognition of the inherent dignity, the equal and inalienable rights of all human beings.

On December 10th not only should the Universal Declaration of Human Rights be published in whole or in part in our daily and weekly newspapers and journals, but also proper use should be made of all other forms of mass communications, particularly radio and television. The fundamental principles of the Declaration need to be supported through community meetings and panel discussions. Religious groups and voluntary civic organizations ought to take hold of several of these basic principles of the Declaration and make them known boldly during the week of December 10th. And, since in this kind of a world, realism is called for, the whole story of human rights and fundamental freedoms should be told, the negative side as well as the significant advances. Besides, it ought to be the purpose of every public relations committee or person promoting Human Rights Day to have a positive point of view and to do everything possible to advance in the community and in the nation and throughout the world the great causes represented in the Universal Declaration of Human Rights.

The International Year for Human Rights

In 1963 the General Assembly of the United Nations voted to designate 1968 as the International Year for Human Rights, and in 1965 and again in 1966 it adopted the resolutions on the International Year for Human Rights, presented here in outline form.

In these resolutions the UN General Assembly outlined certain goals for the International Year for Human Rights.

1. It urged nations which are members of the UN "to take appropriate measures in preparation for the International Year for Human Rights, and in particular to emphasize the urgent need to eliminate discrimination and other violations of human dignity, with special attention to the abolition of racial discrimination and in particular the policy of apartheid."
2. It invited all member nations to ratify "the conventions already concluded in the field of human rights."

3. It invited member nations of the UN to consider, in connection with the year, "the possible advantage of undertaking, on a regional basis, common studies in order to establish more effective protection of human rights."
4. It invited regional intergovernmental organizations with competence in the field to hold an international conference on human rights.
5. It invited the Commission on the Status of Women to participate and cooperate "at every stage" in the preparatory work for the International Year for Human Rights.
6. It also "recommended" that, in view of the historic importance of the observance of the year, UNESCO "should be urged to mobilize the finest resources of culture and art in order to lend the International Year for Human Rights, through literature, music, dance, cinema, television and all other forms and media of communication, a truly universal character."
7. It "decided" that in order to carry out the principles of the Declaration, member nations should convene an International Conference on Human Rights in 1968 which would (a) review the progress that has been made in human rights; (b) evaluate the effectiveness of the materials of the UN in this area; and (c) formulate and prepare a program of further measures to be taken after 1968.
8. It adopted a program of measures and activities which it recommended should be undertaken in 1968 by state (national) members, the United Nations, the specialized agencies, regional intergovernmental organizations and governmental organizations.

Human Rights Day Checklist

The United States National Commission for UNESCO has prepared a checklist especially for teachers, which can also be adapted by other leaders in the community. Because of its value it is reproduced here in its entirety.

Human Rights Day Checklist for Teachers

Teachers and educators everywhere recognize the value of starting to teach respect for the rights of others and the fundamentals of good citizenship in the elementary grades. They are also aware that this type of instruction is fruitful only if the teacher is familiar with the principles upon which our liberties and responsibilities are predicated.

This is true to an even greater extent for teachers who wish to make the UN Universal Declaration of Human Rights a meaningful document for their pupils. The teacher must find ways in which the child can experience, rather than merely verbalize, the meaning of the concepts which are expressed in the UN Universal Declaration of Human Rights and the U.S. Constitution and the Declaration of Independence. These principles can be applied to situations which arise as a result of the child's everyday interaction with his schoolmates.

The UN Universal Declaration of Human Rights itself, if paraphrased in the vocabulary of the grade school student, can be defined and analyzed as it bears on experience in the school and the home.

Class or school programs can help to arouse interest in the Declaration as well as to provide for the child a clearer picture of his own rights and responsibilities. Listed below are a number of activities which have been conducted by schools and teachers as part of Human Rights Day programs. You may find among them some suggestions which may be helpful in planning and executing your Human Rights Day observance.

1. Have an assembly period featuring a well-known authority on human rights. A clergyman or local official might be willing to participate. A question-and-answer period might follow.
2. Ask students to write a report on what human rights mean to them in their community. See if their parents might help by explaining how it affects them in their jobs. Perhaps the parents might wish to participate in a discussion of human rights in the classroom or in an assembly session.
3. Discuss the United Nations and its work in human rights during classes in history, civics, or social studies.

4. Have a class panel discussion to compare the UN Universal Declaration of Human Rights and the U.S. Bill of Rights.

5. Arrange for a showing of a film on human rights. Perhaps you might wish to use it as a topic for a panel discussion later.

6. Review the Four Freedoms and discuss the portions of the Universal Declaration that express similar convictions.

7. Develop a display of appropriate posters and publications. Include as many reproductions of famous documents of freedom as possible.

8. Have the class prepare a skit pointing up the necessity for respect for the rights of others.

9. Promote a contest in the class or throughout the school for the best poster, painting or drawing depicting human rights. Have an exhibit of all the entries. Perhaps local merchants, clubs, or businesses might wish to donate prizes.

10. How about an essay or poetry contest about human rights? Interested groups in the community might be willing to award prizes for the best entries in each age group. The awarding and reading of the winning entries might form the nucleus of a school assembly period.

Program of Measures and Activities

During 1968 special messages will be released by officials of the UN, the executive heads of UN special agencies, the Executive Director of UNICEF, and the executive secretaries of the regional economic commissions, calling attention to the Universal Declaration of Human Rights. Local public relations personnel should anticipate them and tie into them through local mass media.

Moreover, these other items should be utilized:

1. a human rights stamp;
2. the dissemination of the Universal Declaration of Human Rights itself;
3. a special pamphlet on the Declaration published by the United Nations;
4. a radio documentary script on the Declaration;
5. posters;
6. lectures and articles;

7. special display of relevant UN documents.
8. For Human Rights Day, December 10, 1968, it is recommended by the General Assembly that at UN headquarters there be
   (a) a special meeting to commemorate the twentieth anniversary of the Declaration,
   (b) a UN concert, with the widest kind of radio and TV coverage.
9. It is also recommended that the UN award a prize or prizes on December 10, 1968. "If one prize is to be awarded, it should be for outstanding achievements in the field of human rights. If two prizes are to be awarded, one should be for outstanding achievements with reference to the promotion and protection of civil and political rights, and the other for outstanding achievements with reference to the promotion and protection of economic, social and cultural rights. If more than one prize is awarded, each prize should be equal in every way."

It is expected that the human relations prizes (first given on December 10, 1968) will thereafter be presented at five-year intervals.

Government Programs Recommended

For those in charge of promoting special UN programs on the local level the following items, which have been suggested for national governments and which may be adapted in full or in part, ought to be kept in mind so that local events can be coordinated with them:

1. a formal proclamation;
2. special messages reaffirming faith in the dignity and worth of the human person;
3. appointment of *ad hoc* committees to coordinate special events;
4. work for the ratification of international covenants;
5. maintenance of contact with UN specialized agencies;
6. issuance of human rights stamps or special cancellations;
7. dissemination of the Universal Declaration of Human Rights document and message in every possible way;
8. the holding of a special meeting, on the highest possible

level, to commemorate the twentieth anniversary of the Universal Declaration on December 10, 1968.

Cooperation by Non-Governmental Agencies

Because the specific recommendations being sent to non-governmental and voluntary agencies are so important to a successful promotion of the International Year for Human Rights, they are given here at some length.

1. Have all organizations with an interest in human rights participate in the Year.
2. Get these organizations to use the Declaration (or some part of it) as the theme for their annual meeting.
3. Organize special events around Human Rights Day, December 10.
4. Prepare printed matter on the Declaration.
5. Plan community projects (panel discussions, study groups, parades, and school events, for example).
6. Help mold public opinion in favor of the Declaration.
7. Publish historic bills, orations, and documents related to human rights.
8. Encourage radio and television to carry special programs on the Declaration.
9. Suggest that editors of newspapers and popular magazines write special editorials on the Declaration.
10. Have libraries display books related to human rights.
11. Secure active support from churches and church schools.
12. Recommend public discussion or debates on the issues involved in securing human rights and fundamental freedoms.
13. See that all fifty states have special events in recognition of the twentieth anniversary of the Universal Declaration of Human Rights.
14. Use this book widely to help various organizations in your community understand the meaning of the Declaration.

Promotional Suggestions for Voluntary Organizations

The secret of good promotion is to present attractively, through various forms of mass media, a great cause (like the UN and its Declaration of Human Rights) in an up-to-date, relevant way.

This book contains a digest of the vast amount of source material which can be secured from the United Nations itself, through denominational and international public relations offices and such interdenominational offices as Church Women United, and through UNA–USA and other voluntary agencies. The gist of this material in the hands of a competent public relations director in every local community (presented from a constructive point of view) can work wonders for the causes represented in the UN Universal Declaration of Human Rights.

Moreover, when such material is prepared according to the acceptable norms of a local newspaper office, or a local radio or TV station, it has a good chance of being used. And, of course, this is what counts—not the material prepared, or the amount of copy or articles or releases sent out, but the number that is actually used. Therefore, every local public relations director responsible for promoting the causes represented in the Universal Declaration of Human Rights should not only produce acceptable copy, but be aware of the type of material a specific newspaper or radio or TV station uses and then make sure that the timing is correct. This is most important and this is where many voluntary agencies fail in their publicity. They do not pay enough attention to deadlines. Releases must be timely; they also must be on time. A release that is a day (or sometimes a few minutes) late is just a waste of time and energy. Therefore, when the material is ready for publication every possible effort should be made to get it into the hands of the newspaper or radio or TV station in time to be edited and disseminated. When this is accomplished and the material gets before tens of thousands of people, then the principles of the UN are given a positive opportunity—sometimes against great odds—in the local community. In a world that needs the UN desperately, particularly its basic principles which make for peace, understanding, and goodwill, those who now take the contents of this book and implement them in their own communities will be rendering a lasting service to all mankind. For, as UNESCO says, world peace must begin in the minds of people—people everywhere.

Questions for Discussion

1. What is the significance of Human Rights Day and Human Rights Week?
2. How is the International Year for Human Rights going to be observed by states? By the United States government? By the United Nations?
3. What organizations are the best qualified to promote the International Year for Human Rights?
4. Why should the "other side" of the UN be stressed?
5. What is the best way to get involved in UN causes?
6. Why should the religious institutions have a special concern for the successful observance of special United Nations emphases?
7. What accounts for the vast indifference to the "all-out" observance of Human Rights Day?
8. It has been suggested that the United States create a Commission for International Cooperation on Human Rights, possibly patterned after the U.S. National Commission for UNESCO. What do you think of this idea?

Suggestions for Action

1. Check with state and local authorities to see if they have appointed committees to plan for, and to implement, special UN observances.
2. Advocate that the office of a UN High Commissioner for Human Rights be established.
3. Make sure immediately that all civic and religious organizations in your community are supplied with adequate UN information and materials for the observance of special days, weeks, and years.
4. Form a panel discussion group; hold a public meeting on the possibilities presented in this chapter; get organizations connected with the UNA–USA to support the meeting.
5. Check with the mayor of your town well in advance of Human Rights Day (December 10) to discover if he will issue an official proclamation in observance of the day.
6. Get your local paper to run a feature story on the significance of the International Year for Human Rights.

12. The Importance of Non-Governmental and Voluntary Agencies

---

Everyone has duties to the community in which alone the free and full development of his personality is possible. In the exercise of his rights and freedoms, everyone shall be subject only to such limitations as are determined by law solely for the purpose of securing due recognition and respect for the rights and freedoms of others and of meeting the just requirements of morality, public order and the general welfare in a democratic society.

—From the UN Universal Declaration of Human Rights

As we have already seen in the various chapters of this book the United Nations program, if it is to work, must have the confidence, the loyalty, the active support of "the people." Without this the UN can fast become an empty shell. Moreover, an agency such as UNICEF could not function without the financial support which comes directly from the people.

Eleanor Roosevelt put it this way in a speech she delivered at the first anniversary of the Universal Declaration of Human Rights: "In every land, the people must accept and respect these rights and freedoms in their own communities and in their own lives, and by so doing, create countries, and in time, a world where such freedoms are a reality."

It is significant to note that when the Covenant of the League of Nations was drawn up in 1919 it was the "High Contracting Parties" who were responsible for carrying it out. But when the Charter of the United Nations was drawn up it was *the peoples of all the member nations* who were involved. Its preamble stated, "We, the peoples of the United Nations . . . have resolved to combine our efforts to accomplish these aims." Therefore, it is important that the voice of the people fulfills an essential role in the life and work of the UN and its special agencies.

When the statesmen from fifty-one nations met in San

Francisco to formulate the UN Charter, the United States delegation brought with them representatives from forty-two private citizens' organizations. They were the voices of labor and industry, of the churches, of education, women's groups, professional organizations, and scientific groups. They were there to see that the Charter included an open door for the non-governmental agencies whose membership would have to provide the grass-roots basis for the successful operation of the United Nations.

Speaking much later of the Student Leadership Institute on the United Nations, President Lyndon B. Johnson put it this way:

> Few activities are more important than intelligent participation in the affairs that concern all men and all nations. This means knowing facts. It means knowing and following the political procedures—the rules which assure free discussion, incisive debate and precise decision-making. It means a sympathetic understanding of the viewpoint of others—and ceaseless efforts to achieve compromise and consensus.

The President went on to say that the best way to support the United Nations is to "acquire practical experience" in connection with it. This is what the non-governmental and voluntary agencies provide. And as Ambassador Arthur J. Goldberg, chief U.S. delegate to the United Nations, puts it (in referring to such an agency),

> The agenda of the United Nations is the unfinished business of mankind. Each small inch of progress that is made in this vast undertaking is another step toward the achievement of true peace and the rule of law in the world. I am confident that those who have taken part in this program over the years have gained for themselves, and have been able to convey to others, a more informed understanding of the aims and purposes, and the difficulties too, of our work at the United Nations.

The Role of Non-Governmental Organizations (*NGOs*)

Article 71 of the UN Charter recognizes the potential value of cooperation from non-governmental and voluntary organizations as follows:

The Economic and Social Council may make suitable arrangements for consultation with non-governmental organizations which are concerned with matters within its competence. Such arrangements may be made with international organizations and, where appropriate with national organizations after consultation with the member of the United Nations concerned.

Non-governmental organizations have a relationship with both the Economic and Social Council and the Office of Public Information, and there is a difference in the criteria for membership in each case. While the consultative relationships are more involved than we indicate here, the following outline may be of help.

The Committee on Non-Governmental Organizations of the UN Economic and Social Council met at the United Nations headquarters in New York, March 30–31, 1967, and recommended to the council that it accept a number of applications and re-applications of non-governmental organizations for consultative status. The council has three classes of consultative status members: (1) Category A, granted to organizations which have a basic interest in most activities of the council; (2) Category B, for organizations concerned with only certain specific activities of the council; and (3) inclusion in the Register, granted to organizations connected with the council on an *ad hoc* basis.

Under the direction of the UN Office of Public Information, non-governmental organizations may also be accredited to the United Nations in connection with activities in the information field. This represents an ongoing group, with an executive committee of its own. In this list of organizations are associations of industry and business; worldwide trade union organizations; veterans' groups; leading social welfare and teachers' organizations; cooperative societies; farmers' organizations; international professional associations of newspaper editors and publishers, journalists, engineers, lawyers, doctors, architects; youth associations; and women's organizations. The list also includes Catholic, Jewish, Protestant, Muslim, and other religious groups.

Although these organizations differ greatly, they all must fulfill certain criteria in order to fall within the classification "non-governmental organization." They all must not be established by intergovernmental agreement. Moreover, they must be nonprofit-making organizations with a recognized program and the means whereby to achieve their aims.

Each participating organization may name two delegates and three observers to attend NGO annual conferences (called in cooperation with the UN Office of Public Information) and weekly briefing sessions at the United Nations. An official NGO pass is issued to each so that he can cover as many UN meetings and activities as possible. The basic purposes of NGO are consultation regarding the affairs of the United Nations, dissemination of information about the UN, and mobilization of public opinion in matters of mutual concern. In order to keep each organization constantly informed of developments in the fields of UN activity, the Office of Public Information serves as a continuing liaison between the UN and NGO members. A lounge provided for NGO representatives is stocked with UN press releases, documents, and periodicals as well as pamphlets produced by some of the specialized agencies.

The NGOs respond by helping distribute UN informational material, in many cases reproducing it at their own expense. They also organize observances of United Nations Day and Human Rights Day, by promoting activities in support of the specialized agencies and such causes as the Freedom from Hunger Campaign and the International Year for Human Rights. They also help to enlarge contacts with the people in the countries of their operation in behalf of the United Nations.

Obviously the various citizen's groups have forged a powerful link between their millions of members and the UN. When members of the NGOs bring news about the UN to the people "back home" they create a sense of something wider than clan, community, or even nation. And when the NGOs bring pressure upon governments to ratify international covenants, or to pass laws carrying out the standards of an international declaration like the Universal Declaration for Human Rights, they help create a sense of responsibility to the world community.

The United Nations Association of the U.S.A. (*UNA–USA*)

According to Porter McKeever, executive secretary of UNA–USA,

> The United Nations Association of the United States (UNA–USA) is the *only private institution* concentrating on objective, policy-oriented research on the United Nations and other international organizations that, at the same time, has within it the means for nationwide dissemination of its own work and that of others with similar interests. It is independent, private, non-partisan.

It was established in 1964 by a merger between the American Association for the United Nations and the United States Committee for the United Nations. It is composed of individual members, chapters, and a Council of Member Organizations. It is a member of the World Federation of United Nations Associations, one of the international organizations entitled to special privileges before the UN Economic and Social Council.

With chapters in over two hundred communities UNA–USA has more than a hundred major national organizations formally associated with its Council of Organizations.

Some of the activities of UNA–USA, according to Mr. McKeever, are as follows:

Some five thousand high schools participate in an annual contest based on a study unit and examination on United Nations affairs. The Collegiate Council for the United Nations has units on more than four hundred college campuses. Model UN General Assemblies involve hundreds more high schools and colleges. And the number of individual members and subscribers to UNA publications is growing.

There are now many thousands of members in the 120 national voluntary organizations associated with UNA–USA, and this provides a generous allowance for overlap. This cooperative alliance of national organizations, which constitutes a unique and important nationwide educational network, reaches out through publications and local units into hundreds of communities.

Presidents of the United States, since 1948, have issued

proclamations designating October 24 as United Nations Day. They have called upon governors and mayors to take similar action. UNA-USA has, in various ways, implemented these calls to support the United Nations in its work for peace around the world.

With the aid of the Advertising Council, which is the public service agency of the advertising industry, UNA–USA promotes an extensive information program on the United Nations. It provides editorial support and finances the direct costs of producing plates for magazines and newspaper inserts, films and tapes for television and radio, and printing for car cards and outdoor billboards. The time and space are contributed by the media themselves.

In such ways the basic purpose of UNA–USA—"to study and promote the fundamental bases of peace with justice and the international organizations necessary for their development"—is carried out.

Marya Mannes, writing in *VISTA** (July-August 1966) indicates in a few words how important to the UN the support of the people really is:

> . . . the United Nations is no lofty abstraction, no verbal saraband, no plot, no abortive dream. It is a living, flawed reality. It is people—hard-working, committed, responsible human beings. So are we, or should be.
>
> Together we make humanity. Separated, we will destroy it. Spreading this word is what each of us can do for all of us.

The U.S. National Commission for UNESCO and Other Agencies

While the U.S. National Commission for UNESCO (associated with the U.S. State Department) has a special interest in promoting the interests of education, science, and culture in relation to the United Nations, there are also a score or more agencies (religious, community, fraternal) doing magnificent work for the United Nations as a whole as well as for particular phases of it.

The U.S. National Commission for UNESCO (established by act of Congress July 30, 1946) serves as the liaison be-

* The official magazine of UNA–USA.

tween UNESCO per se and the American public. Its chief function is to interpret the extensive work of UNESCO and to achieve support for its basic educational, scientific, and cultural principles. Composed of citizens with special interests in these three areas, and administered through the U.S. State Department, it develops literature and programs which help bring UNESCO, human rights, and the UN at large into the public schools and directly into the community.

Through the Church Center at the UN, many denominations, mainly through leadership of the National Council of Churches, come into first-hand contact with the actual operation of the United Nations. The Center's continual series of on-the-spot seminars is of particular value.

Many interdenominational and interfaith agencies have special departments which constantly promote the interests of the UN and human rights. Space does not permit even the listing of these, but Church Women United (a division of the National Council of Churches which has hundreds of units all over the country); the International Affairs Department of the National Council of Churches; Jewish organizations, especially women's divisions of Jewish organizations; and Roman Catholic agencies are doing a splendid job of promoting UN interests—human rights in particular. The National Women's League of the United Synagogue of America, and the Women's Branch of the Union of Orthodox Jewish Congregations of America, deserve special mention. Other Jewish agencies doing outstanding work in behalf of UN principles include the National Community Relations Advisory Council, the Synagogue Council of America, B'nai B'rith, and the American Jewish Congress (its President, Morris B. Abram, is U.S. delegate on the UN Commission on Human Rights).

The National Congress of Parents and Teachers, because of its *Handbook on the United Nations* and other material and activities, has won for itself special merit.

The YMCA and the YWCA, due to their relationship to international affairs and human rights, rank high among the voluntary organizations supporting the fundamental principles of the UN.

The YWCA in its "National Public Affairs Program 1967–1970" has this to say about basic individual rights and liberties:

Because freedom is indivisible the rights of all depend upon their being guaranteed to each member of the whole society, regardless of sex, race, economic status, or difference of belief or opinion. We have, therefore, supported the preservation and full realization of our traditional civil liberties, equal justice before the law for all individuals, and the protection of citizens in the exercise of their civil rights, protesting vigorously wherever fundamental freedoms are abridged or denied.

While the entire Roman Catholic Church supports the United Nations in specific ways—consider, for example, Pope John's *Pacem in Terris* and Pope Paul's visit to the UN—the Catholic organization in the United States which is probably the most active in promoting UN causes is the National Council of Catholic Women.

Other voluntary agencies, most of which are giving the UN and the cause of human rights special attention, are official members of the United Nations Association of the U.S.A. and of NGOs. When the United Nations comes under attack, it is encouraging to turn to these listings, realizing that a great host of people around the world believe in, and faithfully support, the peace-making functions represented by the "other side" of the United Nations.

Due to the fact that the above listing of agencies is only an example and does not represent the entire list of organizations working in behalf of the UN, the reader is urged to contact the organizations with which he is associated and get material they publish on the United Nations in general and human rights in particular. Involvement in the work of the United Nations and its specialized agencies can be one of the most rewarding experiences of a lifetime.

Questions for Discussion

1. What is the place and function of non-governmental agencies in connection to the UN?
2. How do the non-governmental agencies contribute to the UN?
3. What is the purpose and services rendered by the United Nations Association of the U.S.A.?

4. What part do people at the grass-roots level play in the support of the United Nations?
5. How do the public schools provide an outlet for UN activities?
6. Why is there so much misunderstanding of, and opposition to, the United Nations?

Suggestions for Action

1. Find out what the John Birch Society thinks of the United Nations.
2. Check with the American Jewish Committee to discover what it means when it recommends that "universities and non-governmental organizations take a more active part in a world-wide education, research and study program in human rights."
3. Eleanor Roosevelt said, "Without concerted citizen action to uphold these rights close to home, we shall look in vain for progress in the larger world." By speech and action give this idea your support.
4. Form a panel discussion group; hold a public meeting on the question of how well your community is organized to support the International Human Rights Year; get organizations connected with the UNA–USA to support the meeting and report on their work.
5. Join a (local) UNA–USA group if you do not already belong.
6. Have a big anniversary celebration in your community observing the twentieth anniversary of the UN Universal Declaration of Human Rights, getting the cooperation of school, church, and civic groups affiliated with the UNA–USA.

UNIVERSAL DECLARATION OF HUMAN RIGHTS

Preamble

Whereas recognition of the inherent dignity and of the equal and inalienable rights of all members of the human family is the foundation of freedom, justice and peace in the world.

Whereas disregard and contempt for human rights have resulted in barbarous acts which have outraged the conscience of mankind, and the advent of a world in which human beings shall enjoy freedom of speech and belief and freedom from fear and want has been proclaimed as the highest aspiration of the common people,

Whereas it is essential, if man is not to be compelled to have recourse, as a last resort, to rebellion against tyranny and oppression, that human rights should be protected by the rule of law,

Whereas it is essential to promote the development of friendly relations between nations,

Whereas the peoples of the United Nations have in the Charter reaffirmed their faith in fundamental human rights, in the dignity and worth of the human person and in the equal rights of men and women and have determined to promote social progress and better standards of life in larger freedom,

Whereas Member States have pledged themselves to achieve, in cooperation with the United Nations, the promotion of universal respect for and observance of human rights and fundamental freedoms,

Whereas a common understanding of these rights and freedoms is of the greatest importance for the full realization of this pledge,

Now therefore

THE GENERAL ASSEMBLY proclaims

This Universal Declaration of Human Rights as a common standard of achievement for all peoples and all nations, to the end that every individual and every organ of society, keeping this Declaration constantly in mind, shall strive by teaching and education to promote respect for these rights and freedoms and by progressive measures, national and international, to secure their universal and effective recognition and observance, both among the peoples of Member States themselves and among the peoples of territories under their jurisdiction.

Article 1. All human beings are born free and equal in dignity and rights. They are endowed with reason and conscience and should act towards one another in a spirit of brotherhood.

Article 2. Everyone is entitled to all the rights and freedoms set forth in this Declaration, without distinction of any kind, such as race, colour, sex, language, religion, political or other opinion, national or social origin, property, birth or other status. Furthermore, no distinction shall be made on the basis of the political, jurisdictional or international status of the country or territory to which a person belongs, whether it be independent, trust, non-self-governing or under any other limitation of sovereignty.

Article 3. Everyone has the right to life, liberty and security of person.

Article 4. No one shall be held in slavery or servitude; slavery and the slave trade shall be prohibited in all their forms.

Article 5. No one shall be subjected to torture or to cruel, inhuman or degrading treatment or punishment.

Article 6. Everyone has the right to recognition everywhere as a person before the law.

Article 7. All are equal before the law and are entitled without any discrimination to equal protection of the law. All are entitled to equal protection against any discrimination in violation of this Declaration and against any incitement to such discrimination.

Article 8. Everyone has the right to an effective remedy by the competent national tribunals for acts violating the fundamental rights granted him by the constitution or by law.

Article 9. No one shall be subjected to arbitrary arrest, detention or exile.

Article 10. Everyone is entitled in full equality to a fair and public hearing by an independent and impartial tribunal, in the determination of his rights and obligations and of any criminal charge against him.

Article 11. (1) Everyone charged with a penal offence has the right to be presumed innocent until proved guilty according to law in a public trial at which he has had all the guarantees necessary for his defence.

(2) No one shall be held guilty of any penal offence on account of any act or omission which did not constitute a penal offence, under

national or international law, at the time when it was committed. Nor shall a heavier penalty be imposed than the one that was applicable at the time the penal offence was committed.

Article 12. No one shall be subjected to arbitrary interference with his privacy, family, home or correspondence, nor to attacks upon his honour and reputation. Everyone has the right to the protection of the law against such interference or attacks.

Article 13. (1) Everyone has the right to freedom of movement and residence within the borders of each state.
(2) Everyone has the right to leave any country, including his own, and to return to his country.

Article 14. (1) Everyone has the right to seek and to enjoy in other countries asylum from persecution.
(2) This right may not be invoked in the case of prosecutions genuinely arising from non-political crimes or from acts contrary to the purposes and principles of the United Nations.

Article 15. (1) Everyone has the right to a nationality.
(2) No one shall be arbitrarily deprived of his nationality nor denied the right to change his nationality.

Article 16. (1) Men and women of full age, without any limitation due to race, nationality or religion, have the right to marry and to found a family. They are entitled to equal rights as to marriage, during marriage and at its dissolution.
(2) Marriage shall be entered into only with the free and full consent of the intending spouses.
(3) The family is the natural and fundamental group unit of society and is entitled to protection by society and the State.

Article 17. (1) Everyone has the right to own property alone as well as in association with others.
(2) No one shall be arbitrarily deprived of his property.

Article 18. Everyone has the right to freedom of thought, conscience and religion; this right includes freedom to change his religion or belief, and freedom, either alone or in community with others and in public or private, to manifest his religion or belief in teaching, practice, worship and observance.

Article 19. Everyone has the right to freedom of opinion and expression; this right includes freedom to hold opinions without interference and to seek, receive and impart information and ideas through any media and regardless of frontiers.

Article 20. (1) Everyone has the right to freedom of peaceful assembly and association.
(2) No one may be compelled to belong to an association.

Article 21. (1) Everyone has the right to take part in the government of his country, directly or through freely chosen representatives.
(2) Everyone has the right of equal access to public service in his country.
(3) The will of the people shall be the basis of the authority of government; this will shall be expressed in periodic and genuine elections which shall be by universal and equal suffrage and shall be held by secret vote or by equivalent free voting procedures.

Article 22. Everyone, as a member of society, has the right to social security and is entitled to realization, through national effort and international co-operation and in accordance with the organization and resources of each State, of the economic, social and cultural rights indispensable for his dignity and the free development of his personality.

Article 23. (1) Everyone has the right to work, to free choice of employment, to just and favorable conditions of work and to protection against unemployment.
(2) Everyone, without any discrimination, has the right to equal pay for equal work.
(3) Everyone who works has the right to just and favorable remuneration insuring for himself and his family an existence worthy of human dignity, and supplemented, if necessary, by other means of social protection.
(4) Everyone has the right to form and to join trade unions for the protection of his interests.

Article 24. Everyone has the right to rest and leisure, including reasonable limitation of working hours and periodic holidays with pay.

Article 25. (1) Everyone has the right to a standard of living adequate for the health and well-being of himself and of his family, including food, clothing, housing and medical care and necessary social services, and the right to security in the event of unemployment, sickness, disability, widowhood, old age or other lack of livelihood in circumstances beyond his control.
(2) Motherhood and childhood are entitled to special care and assistance. All children, whether born in or out of wedlock, shall enjoy the same social protection.

Article 26. (1) Everyone has the right to education. Education shall be free, at least in the elementary and fundamental stages. Elementary education shall be compulsory. Technical and professional education shall be made generally available and higher education shall be equally accessible to all on the basis of merit.
(2) Education shall be directed to the full development of the

human personality and to the strengthening of respect for human rights and fundamental freedoms. It shall promote understanding, tolerance and friendship among all nations, racial or religious groups, and shall further the activities of the United Nations for the maintenance of peace.
(3) Parents have a prior right to choose the kind of education that shall be given to their children.

Article 27. (1) Everyone has the right freely to participate in the cultural life of the community, to enjoy the arts and to share in scientific advancement and its benefits.
(2) Everyone has the right to the protection of the moral and material interests resulting from any scientific, literary or artistic production of which he is the author.

Article 28. Everyone is entitled to a social and international order in which the rights and freedoms set forth in this Declaration can be fully realized.

Article 29. (1) Everyone has duties to the community in which alone the free and full development of his personality is possible.
(2) In the exercise of his rights and freedoms, everyone shall be subject only to such limitations as are determined by law solely for the purpose of securing due recognition and respect for the rights and freedoms of others and of meeting the just requirements of morality, public order and the general welfare in a democratic society.
(3) These rights and freedoms may in no case be exercised contrary to the purposes and principles of the United Nations.

Article 30. Nothing in this Declaration may be interpreted as implying for any State, group or person any right to engage in any activity or to perform any act aimed at the destruction of any of the rights and freedoms set forth herein.